MW01068338

Experiencing Sound

Experiencing Sound

THE SENSATION OF BEING

Lawrence Kramer

UNIVERSITY OF CALIFORNIA PRESS

University of California Press
Oakland, California

© 2024 by Lawrence Kramer

Library of Congress Cataloging-in-Publication Data

Names: Kramer, Lawrence, author.
Title: Experiencing sound : the sensation of being / Lawrence Kramer.
Description: Oakland, California : University of California Press, [2024]
    | Includes bibliographical references and index.
Identifiers: LCCN 2023057042 (print) | LCCN 2023057043 (ebook) |
    ISBN 9780520400849 (cloth) | ISBN 9780520400856 (ebook)
Subjects: LCSH: Sounds—Philosophy. | Music—Philosophy and
    aesthetics. | Sounds—Social aspects.
Classification: LCC B105.S59 K725 2024 (print) | LCC B105.S59 (ebook) |
    DDC 121/.35—dc23/eng/20240109
LC record available at https://lccn.loc.gov/2023057042
LC ebook record available at https://lccn.loc.gov/2023057043

Manufactured in the United States of America

33 32 31 30 29 28 27 26 25 24
10 9 8 7 6 5 4 3 2

Contents

Preface

This book grew out of my increasing awareness, over many years of writing about music and also composing it, that music is made of sound. The fact may seem perfectly obvious, but it has perhaps been too obvious for its own good. Our customary ways of thinking about music pay too little heed to it. Because music disappears in the act of being made or heard, we cling to the vestiges it leaves behind. What reaches our ears as a passing sensation ends up in our minds as a fictional object. Grasping the object, we mute the sound, even in the act of describing it. There is probably no way to avoid this altogether, but there is a way to get beyond it. We can learn to hear music as a temporary cut in a vast continuous flow of sound. Once we do that, the concepts of both sound and music undergo substantial change. The boundaries between them blur. It becomes possible, and comes to feel necessary, to listen to the flow of sound as we listen to music and to hear in music the flow of sound at work.

My previous study of sound, *The Hum of the World*, makes a start on that listening and that hearing. The book is guided by the aphorism that sound is the measure of life. It gathers evidence for the essential vitality of sound from numerous sources ancient and modern, including music, philosophy, science, and literature. *Experiencing Sound* adopts the same premise and continues the effort to give sound its due. It also, as it must, moves in new directions, two of them in particular:

First, sound in these pages is understood not just as something we sense but as something we need. The need is not practical, though it is that, too, but existential, ontological. Sound is the medium we dwell in. It is the one sense we cannot cease to use.

Second, sound directs our passage through time. It shapes our orientation to the future moment and also to the moment when the future stops. If sound is the measure of life, its end must be a measure of death. The delicate balance of vitality and mortality is a recurrent theme in the reflections to follow.

If "reflections" is the right word. I'm not sure we have the right vocabulary to describe the kind of book this is, though the book's form is hardly novel. It is modeled on the loose assembly of observations, thoughts, interpretations, and the like found, for example, in the writings of three of my favorite thinkers: Nietzsche, the later Wittgenstein, and Barthes. Such writing embodies a form of thinking equally devoted to the demands of reasonable argument and the necessity for conceptual and verbal invention, for metaphor, provocation, and risk. There is also a personal element which should be understood as a genuine conceptual resource. As to what to call the various entries, I suppose "reflections" or "observations" will have to do, but perhaps they are better thought of as forays, forays in the sense of ventures, but even to some degree in the military sense, what T. S. Eliot called "raids on the inarticulate." Perhaps the foray should be recognized as a genre of thought.

Like *The Hum of the World, Experiencing Sound* can be read more or less at random. The brevity and the principle of the forays see to that. Some threads run through adjoining segments; others recur at wider intervals. But in keeping with its theme of passing time, *Experiencing Sound* follows a long arc. The ideal way to read it may be straight through. Reader's choice, as always.

Introduction

Sound in recent years has escaped its traditionally subordinate relationship to sight and become the object of widespread interest. Sound studies is a flourishing field. Much of the work done under this rubric has concentrated either on the technological history of sound or on the social uses and abuses of sound.[1] In my book *The Hum of the World: A Philosophy of Listening* (2019), I sought to focus on the ways in which sound has been imagined and represented in Western culture.[2] The meaning of sound depends on how it is apprehended. We need the work on technology and social impact, but we also need work on how sound has been experienced—felt, remembered, and conceived. More attention is still needed to the way sound frames our relationship to the world and forms the measure of life. Of course there is a great deal of overlap among sonic spheres of interest. But to be very clear: sound as studied here is auditory rather than acoustic. It is fully material but always mediated by human sensation, perception, feeling, and understanding. It is sound as lived.

If we think of hearing as an involuntary physical event and of listening as purposive, we might say that the primary condition of sound is the transformation of hearing into listening. (This would be true of any creature with ears.) The process is continuous, so much so that the distinction on which it is based melts away more often than not. This transformation is not just something that happens but something we do. It is a fundamentally creative process that goes beyond its social, physical, and material sources. It is how we live with sound and live through sound and it is the subject raised in *The Hum of the World* and continued here.

The Hum of the World is grounded in a new concept and in a principle associated with it. The concept is the hum of my title, which also, for convenience, goes by the name of the *audiable*—the word *audible* enriched with a resonant extra vowel sound. The audiable is the faint continuous background sound that accompanies all of our sensory perception. This sound on rare occasions becomes perceptible and meaningful. Most of the time it hovers on the fringes of perception where, however, it does essential work for us. It forms a barrier against total silence, dead silence, a condition that we rarely experience and that disturbs us greatly when we do. When the world goes totally silent, we often listen to our bodies instead, the pulse in our veins, the air in our lungs. We need to hear *something*.

The continuity of the audiable assures us of the continuity of our experience of the world, which is to say, the continuation of life. This is the principle that goes with the concept. The audiable is not only a sound you may sometimes hear. It is also the sound of what you are about to hear, the sound that tells you that something else is coming.

For sound is always directed toward the future. It starts just before it is heard but it is heard in the passage from *now* to *next* that constitutes the immediate present. Its link to the future is so strong that sound is the sensory medium in which the awareness of coming time is felt. More particularly, sound is the sensory medium in which the awareness of continuing life is felt. Although we customarily speak of looking into the future, in practical everyday terms what we do is listen to the future arriving. The audiable is the felt promise of sound, of more sound, and therefore, most fundamentally, of more life.

We do not normally hear the audiable in the usual sense of "hear," but it is a genuine auditory phenomenon within the sense of hearing. For a visual analogy, we might turn to things seen best when we concentrate on them mentally but observe them only from the corner of the eye, with peripheral vision. Such averted vision makes faint objects more discernible. The star cluster known as the Pleiades offers a good example. It is almost invisible if you try to stare at it, but evocatively present if you look askance. The audiable is usually best observed with what we might call averted hearing. Its presence resonates through other sounds at or near the threshold of audibility that temporarily blend with it.

If these faint sounds hover over what we listen to, they form an aura or haze that merges with the universal background. If the sounds are exposed so we hear them falling away, we can also hear the hum of the world rising to take them in. For a passing moment we can catch the tone of the audiable. Another visual analogy may prove helpful. The ephemeral sound is like a drop of dye falling into a glass of water. For a moment the water takes on a swirl of coloration; one can see its liquidity; then the color dissipates and the water's translucency returns, a little altered. Because sound, unlike sight, has the capacity to ebb and flow, it often attracts metaphors of running or falling water. This affinity is so close that it is hard to think of sound without it. The analogy to the drop of dye may be colorful but it is not entirely visual; it speaks to the auditory undercurrent of experience.

The audiable has a rich but largely neglected history in Western thought, science, and art dating from the late classical era if not before. Once we begin to seek them out, the workings of the audiable and the articulation of life through sound turn up everywhere. They make available kinds of knowledge and pleasure that have been veiled—everywhere— by the normative domination of the visual as the medium of understanding. And "everywhere" is the point, because the audiable is essential to our sense of connection with reality. The audiable is not something we hear because it is there. It is something that is there because we hear it.

Henry James's novel *The American,* written in 1876, offers a literally striking example. In the course of making a new friend, the novel's hero hears something—*hears* something—in the face he looks at: "The great point in his face was that it was intensely alive—frankly, ardently, gallantly alive. The look of it was like a bell, of which the handle might have been in the young man's soul: at a touch of the handle it rang with a loud silver sound."[3]

Two aspects of this description are especially noteworthy. First, the measure of the face's intense aliveness is an imaginary sound. The resonance of the bell extends the general sense of aliveness into vivid particulars: frankness, ardor, gallantry. The young man's face is experienced through an auditory gaze. Second, because the sound is a bell sound, its silver ring has a quality that we can attend to as a metaphor and also listen to in the mind's ear. The sound is one that will linger first and then gradually fade until it reaches, then crosses, the threshold of audibility. When it reaches that threshold, it merges into the general background of all hearing for which *The Hum of the World* is named.

A more recent illustration occurs in Anthony Doerr's short story "The Caretaker." The protagonist, an African immigrant in California, tries at one point to imagine what it must be like to be deaf. Frustrated by his failures to understand the cultural and racial cues addressed to him, he decides to shut them out. He supposes—incorrectly—that deafness consists of "a kind of void, a nothingness, an oblivion." But when he tries to deafen himself by clamping his hands over his ears, he fails, and fails necessarily: "There is always noise, the flux and murmur of his body's machinery, a hum in his head."[4]

This description traces a subtle progression. Noise is external and meaningless; the flux and murmur of the body's machinery is internal and meaningful. The body as machinery may feel alienated, but the listener knows how the machinery works, and the movement from flux to murmur arrives at the threshold of speech. From there the progression moves to the hum in the head, which is pervasive and indeterminate. Is it internal or external? Is it the hum of impending thought or language or something else? Whatever it is, it fills the space between the ears, the seat of the sense of hearing. The hum is *in* the protagonist's head but not necessarily *of* it. Like the sound of James's bell it merges into the hum of the world. And in so doing it blocks him—saves him—from the oblivion he seeks.

But what if the listener had actually been deaf? It must be acknowledged that this book assumes the perspective of a hearing person, and that the heard world is its subject. The same goes for *The Hum of the World*. I do not presume to speak for the deaf community, but it is nonetheless clear that sound plays a fundamental role in the lives of the deaf. But it plays that role on their terms. Music, especially, is a part of deaf culture, grasped by means of vibration, touch, rhythm, and a form of singing in which the hands, signing, with a style and rhythm of their own, do the work that the voice cannot do. More generally, where the ears stop, the body opens other channels for sound.[5] The true exception to the rule of sound may come from hearing not too little but too much: from tinnitus, ringing in the ears; from hyperacusis, the perception of all sound as too loud; or from misophonia, an inexplicable aversion to specific sounds. Sometimes we are at the mercy of our ears.

. . . . .

This sequel to *The Hum of the World* is a slowly cumulating series of short studies. In continuing to ask how we apprehend sound in a multitude of settings, it keeps returning, almost as if involuntarily, to the effects of sound on the experience of being finite: exposed, vulnerable, transient. The guiding thread is the need I spoke of earlier, the need to hear something rather than nothing. Sound makes life audible, says *The Hum of the World,* and so says the hum that is its namesake. Being audible belongs to the very concept of life. But this audibility, says *Experiencing Sound,* is more than simply a phenomenon to enjoy or ponder. It is the answer to a demand, an imperative, an urge. Its value goes beyond pleasure and knowledge, though it may bring both. There are times when sound is not only the measure of life but also the means of upholding it. It may be a lifeline for an enslaved person hidden for seven years in a crawlspace; it may be the lifespan of a musical work meant to play continuously for a thousand years. Both cases appear in these pages along with many others.

Like *The Hum of the World, Experiencing Sound* seeks to show that following the thread of sound can change our understanding of history, language, feeling, and sensation. But *Experiencing Sound* goes a step further by threading in the *need* for sound as an essential dimension of our experience of it. The need is always there. It does not matter whether the experience is blissful or terrible. That we need sound does not always mean we can endure it. It may merit praise not for what it gives but for what it reveals. Still, as some of the entries below should illustrate, there are times and circumstances in which meeting the need for sound is what makes life livable.

Sound does in the world of the senses what telling stories does in the world of thought: it helps us make sense of living in time. Sense and sensation cross and mingle; a story implies a voice and sounds have tales to tell. This is both an everyday matter—the different hours have their different sounds—and one that carries over long, sometimes very long, spans. Whatever the time, the need hums along. Quiet may be sought, but silence must be broken.

1 June 24, 2019

THE WIND ON MARS

Late in 2018 an instrument on a NASA Mars lander "heard" something that nothing and no one on earth had heard before: the sound of the Martian wind. The instrument was designed to take seismographic readings, but a moderate 10- to 15-mile-per-hour wind—technically just a breeze—caused the spacecraft to vibrate, thus turning its recording device into an inadvertent wind phonograph, an interplanetary Aeolian harp. With a technological boost, the instrumental readout could be turned into a sound recording. The Martian wind thus became audible, albeit at one remove, to the human ear.

According to the *New York Times*, Bruce Banerdt, the chief investigator of this Mars mission, said during a news conference that he found the sounds "really unworldly. They do sound like the wind or maybe the ocean kind of roaring in the background. But [the sound] also has an unworldly feel to it."[1] In one sense, of course, the word "unworldly" is superfluous. It is a perfectly literal description of this sound: the wind was blowing on another world. That literal fact, however, is the very reason why the figurative meaning of the word is evocative: the sound is "unworldly" in the sense that it carries us out of our common frame of reference into a mysterious realm, one more unfathomable than the breadth of the ocean. True, the Martian wind does sound the like wind as we know it; how could it not? It was just that, a wind, regardless of the planet it blew on. But this wind also sounds strange in a way that no earth wind could, even if the actual sounds involved were indistinguishable. What we know affects what we hear.

And yet, in another sense, "unworldly" is a poor choice of word here. The faint sound "kind of roaring in the background," a sound like the wind's and the ocean's but not identical to them, links the wind on Mars to the faint background sound that permeates life on earth—to the hum of the world that I have proposed calling the *audiable*. When we hear the faintness and strangeness of this wind on Mars, we also hear its closeness to that enveloping background, without which no wind could sound, whether on Mars or Earth or anywhere else. The wind makes Mars worldly to us in a way that visual and seismic data could not. The sense of the world is auditory, on that planet as well as this. There is no parallel on our nearest celestial neighbor, the moon, which lights the night sky beautifully and mysteriously but is not, for all that, a world. There is no wind on the moon. The sense of a world cannot be established only by what we can see, as we can see the lunar landscape. A planet can be seen, pure and simple. But a world can be seen only if it can be heard.

2 Listening for the Llamas

Anne Carson's prose poem "Short Talk on Homer and John Ashbery" brings its title figures into freewheeling association with each other, with Freud, with dreams, with Adorno, with the classicist Stanley Lombardo, who has translated Homer, and, oh, yes, with llamas. My concern in this entry is mostly with the llamas:

> Down the road from the summer cottage of my friend Stanley Lombardo is a farm where emus and llamas graze. On the fence a sign informs us that "llamas hum to their young." Do not worry, the sign implies, humming is O.K. Does the demographic of dreams emit a worrying sound? . . . Llamas are stately, with an air of deep comedy, and larger than they seem. "You hit one of those you can say goodbye to your car," commented Stanley Lombardo, translator. He also told me that llamas never stop moving their ears even when sleeping.[1]

Llamas do, indeed, hum to their young. Likewise they hum when they're worried. But what are they doing here amid these luminaries of high culture? And what is it with their ears?

The deep comedy of this passage turns on the strange phrase "the demographic of dreams." Just who or what populates dreams, be they our dreams or those of the llamas? The figures we see in dreams are insubstantial, like the shades in the underworld of Homer's *Odyssey* who will not speak unless they receive an offering of blood—precisely what they lack. The demographic of dreams is a community of silence. Speech does occur in dreams but it has no more auditory weight than the visual forms in dreams have bodily substance. The underworld of dreams is populated by shades that move soundlessly and speak with the shades of voices.

But should we worry about this? Should we hear a worried hum from the demographic of dreams as we might from a llama worrying over its young? Or should we accept the assurance of the sign that humming is OK but dreams don't have to worry about it? Perhaps we should be like llamas in their other habit and—figuratively speaking—never stop moving our ears even when sleeping. If there is a worried hum to be dealt with, our ears will let us know. They connect us to the world even when—especially when—we pay them no mind. They hear the world and its hum even when we're sleeping. They assure us that when we dream—and when is that? Surely not only when we sleep—we can follow, for the time, the stately movement of high comedy and what the poem later calls the disposition to "careless joy in almost any situation."

3   Auditory Epiphanies

When a person speaks the truth, more is demanded than that the spoken words be true.[1] They must also carry the ring of truth. Sometimes the truth only feels true when we can hear the sound of it. Merely knowing it is not enough.

Since the middle of the eighteenth century a certain type of visually based knowledge has become increasingly prominent in both science and art. The historian of science Lorraine Daston calls it the *coup d'oeil*, the stroke of the eye: a sudden, irrefutable understanding glimpsed in a moment that brings a multitude of details together as one.[2] Does this visual epiphany have an auditory equivalent, a *coup d'oreille*, or stroke of the ear?

The historical record suggests that the answer is yes, though the auditory form is rarer and more focused than its visual counterpart. It may also be older, and perhaps more elemental. Aeschylus testifies to it in his tragedy *Agamemnon* when the chorus learns of the fall of Troy from a signal fire but does not believe the city has fallen until a messenger has described it, and with eloquence. The sound of the messenger's voice is as weighty as his words.

Probably the most famous example is recorded by St. Augustine in his *Confessions;* I discuss it in detail in *The Hum of the World*. Augustine tells us that while sitting under a fig tree in a wretched, self-accusatory state of mind, and weeping bitterly, he heard the voice of a child chanting the Latin words "Tolle, lege": take up, read. At once he knew what to do. He retrieved a copy of the Bible he had left on a bench and opened it at random. The passage he lit on held another injunction at its core: "Put on the Lord Jesus Christ, and make no provision for the flesh." Augustine's report on the aftermath is unequivocal. His reading, which was silent, corresponded inwardly to the sound of the sudden chant. His entire spiritual history had crystallized in a moment: "I wanted to read no further, nor did I need to. For instantly, as the sentence ended, there was infused in my heart something like the light of full certainty and all the gloom of doubt vanished away."[3]

Augustine's description includes all of the typical features of the *coup d'oreille*. The auditory stroke is sudden, unexpected, and certain (in these respects it resembles its visual cousin); it comes in the sound of a speaking or singing voice; and it takes the form of a command or admonition or injunction. The guiding word tends to be welcome, as it is for Augustine; the guiding voice tends to be aesthetically pleasing, which is implicitly true here of the child's chant. The sheer value of sound is essential to this persuasive (or compelling) pleasure, as Augustine's "tolle, lege" also exemplifies: note the trochaic rhythm of the phrase, the identical closing vowels, the smooth alliteration on the sound of the "l," and the softening of the "t" of "tolle" to the "l" of "lege." The words almost chant themselves on the page. And their appeal, their peal, as sound is not extraneous to the knowledge they impart but essential to it. Their sonority embodies the value of the truth they have to tell.

If it is a truth. For Augustine that is how it felt and it is what he believed. But this reflection on the auditory epiphany would not be complete without the recognition of its dark obverse: the voice that deceives and seduces, the Siren song, the echoes in Plato's cave, the voices in the head that belittle the listener or command acts of violence. Besides, the truth is not always what the listener wants to hear. In what we might call the other most famous example, the sudden voice is neither pleasing nor welcome, which is exactly why its impact is so powerful: "Methought I heard a voice cry, 'Sleep no more! / Macbeth hath murdered sleep.'"

In the tradition represented by these Western examples, truth is not simply a matter of what can be verified empirically or conceived abstractly. It is a matter of what can be sounded. Is it possible that the *sound* of truth will set us free?

4 Sound and World

The hum of the world is a real phenomenon but it is not an objective one. It cannot be detected or measured by instruments. It exists only in our observation of it, both in the moment and over the many centuries of its previously unobserved history. But it may nonetheless have an empirical foundation. An elementary fact about sound is that it does not travel in a vacuum; sound needs an atmosphere through which to travel. But an atmosphere can be found only on a world, which means that sound can exist only in a world. Its existence testifies to the presence of a world. Where sound is, world is; where world is, sound is. Any sound one hears, any sound one might hear, is the sound of whatever emits it. But it is also the sound of a world, the resonance of an enveloping whole with characteristics that change as one dwells in it. The way to reach the audiable, the hum of the only world we live in, is to redirect this general perception to the particulars that support it. It is to ask how sound becomes not the sound of a world that just happens to be ours, but immediately the sound of *the* world and no other. We can ask that question in the expectation of real answers in experience because sound is the sensory ground of world-feeling, of world-perception. Where there is sound, where sound impends, the world unfolds to carry it.

Our most immediate experience of this is one we are destined to forget. It comes in the womb, when hearing develops and the unborn child hears first its mother's heartbeat and then the rumor of a wider world than the one that contains it before birth. Of course the infant's first connection with the world comes in the cry, but although the cry is sent out *into* the world it does not place the infant *in* the world. That role seems reserved for laughter. Modern pediatrics tells us that four-month-old infants begin to laugh at things they perceive. Their laughter stems not from need, like the cry, but from the pleasures of discovery. The world detaches laughter from our bodies and draws us after it.

The philosopher and polymath Julia Kristeva regards the onset of such laughter as a pivotal phase in the transition from the infant's babble to language.[1] Intriguingly, the same idea seems to have occurred to St. Augustine sixteen centuries earlier. Augustine was embarrassed at having been a baby; he regarded infants as selfish little sinners. But the passage from cry to speech intrigued him, and the path went by way of laughter:

At the very first I knew how to suck, to lie quiet when I was full, and to cry when in pain—nothing more. Afterward I began to laugh—at first in my sleep, then when waking. For this I have been told about myself and I believe it—though I cannot remember it—for I see the same things in other infants. Then, little by little, I realized where I was and wished to tell my wishes to those who might satisfy them, but I could not . . . [until,] as my infancy closed, I [began] learning signs by which my feelings could be communicated to others.[2]

In the meantime, little sinner that he was, the infant Augustine—so he tells us—took revenge for not being understood by crying a lot.

5 Listening to Silence

Silence must be broken. However observed, silence must be broken.

But silence is not a single phenomenon and its various forms shade into each other. Except in one case, it is not the absence of sound but a form of sound.

Silence is most often the silence *of* something. It is the sound left behind when another sound stops. It forms an audible gap in the soundscape in which the soundscape may momentarily be swallowed up.

Silence may also be the superlative degree of quiet, a condition in which hearing thins out and we feel no need to listen for anything except, perhaps, for the audiable. The sounds in this living silence are perceived but not observed—except, perhaps, for the audiable. We hear them without being particularly conscious of them.

Dead silence is the exceptional case. It is more a feeling than an acoustic condition. It comes about when we cannot hear even the sounds that reach us. Dead silence puts sound in abeyance. It feels like being abandoned, even by the audiable. By common consent, it really does feel deathly. Dead silence turns listening into the negation of hearing. In normal circumstances listening is a form of hearing, whereas hearing may go on without listening. We don't necessarily listen to what we hear any more than we necessarily hear what we listen for. When we hear nothing, we listen for anything. Dead silence is thwarted listening.

The governess in Henry James's horror story "The Turn of the Screw" discovers as much in her first encounter with the apparition that will turn her world upside down: "It was as if, while I took in, what I did take in, all the rest of the scene had been stricken with death. I can hear again, as I write, the intense hush in which the sounds of evening dropped. The rooks stopped cawing in the golden sky and the friendly hour lost for the unspeakable minute all its voice."[1] This silence is an abyss into which hearing listens to itself drop, not only in the (literally) unspeakable minute but also in the act, long afterward, of recalling it in writing.

Strictly speaking, however, all silence is near silence. For living ears, silence is at worst the minimum of sound. And if it is observed—not in the sense of keeping mum but in the sense of scrutinizing something—then silence too can be heard in relation to life, not death. Silence must be broken, but it does not always need to be broken right away.

Such a spell of observation forms the basis of John Cage's famous but much misunderstood composition *4'33"*.[2] This music is often said to consist of four minutes, thirty-three seconds of silence, that is, of soundlessness. But it consists of anything but that. The composition, which is in three movements (indicated visually), is a frame for otherwise unheard, otherwise unappreciated sound. It is an auditory screen on which faint sounds flit by as if floating on the hum of the world. The music is whatever sounds fill the intervals of time, and each listener hears it differently.

One aim of *4'33"* is to cure the listener of the fear of silence and thus from the need to mask it. Sound may be a means of avoidance; it may keep us from hearing what near silence might reveal—to our dismay. The soprano Julia Bullock enacted a dramatic unmasking of silence during a performance at New York's Metropolitan Museum in January 2018. The program was a tribute to Josephine Baker, the African American entertainer whose dancing made her the toast of Paris during the Jazz Age. Baker spied for the French Resistance during World War II; she subsequently became an important figure in the American civil rights movement. Like Richard Wright and James Baldwin later, Baker sought to escape American racism in France. But even in the nominally welcoming Parisian scene, her work, for all its brilliance, was shadowed by the need to conform to racial stereotypes. Bullock found a way to make that duality audible.

The performance climaxed with a turn from song to dance. As Corinna da Fonseca-Wollheim described it, "When Ms. Bullock broke into movement—flashing almost-bare breasts and quoting some of the angular gestures made famous by Baker—she did so to the accompaniment of total silence, with only the sound of her increasingly labored breath amplified in space."[3] "Total silence" here can only mean *musical* silence. Bullock was dancing on the museum's grand staircase, framed by what can only be described as a reverberant hush. At first such sound as there was came from the audiable, or something very close to it, overlapping with the first susurrations of breath. As the singer-turned-dancer's movements intensified, estranged by the silence of music, her breath sounds became harsh, raw, sometimes guttural. By unmasking the sound of the dancer's bodily labor and initiating it in *near* silence, close to the bone of the audiable, Bullock's performance reclaimed the autonomy of Baker's body. But as her breath became more labored, it also exposed the subjection that Baker had to submit to, precisely in order to dance, to make herself visible, to sing, to make her way. But Bullock, as she notes on her website, was not impersonating Baker; she was, one might say, paraphrasing her in bodily form. By enhancing not only the visibility but also the audibility of her own body, Bullock affirmed herself as the originator of her own breathlessness. "As I walk," she writes, "down the central steps of this institution that holds so much of the complicated, ruthless, and astonishing history of America, I am walking as myself."[4]

6 Calm Sea

GOING NOWHERE, HEARING NOTHING

What happens when dead silence does, after all, accost us? The audiable forms a barrier against that silence; what happens when it fails?

Goethe's little poem "Calm Sea," or "Meeresstille" (1795), tries to capture the absence of both sound and motion. Between 1816 and 1828, this vignette of a sailing ship unable to make progress at sea inspired, first, a song by Schubert; then, with its companion piece "Prosperous Voyage," a brief cantata by Beethoven; and then, again with "Prosperous Voyage," an overture by Mendelssohn.

The poem seems to be asking how language or speech can represent silence, the very condition that language exists to break. Here is my translation in two versions, one based on preserving the sense and the other on preserving the sound. Both seek to retain the key elements of the verses: their word order, their stark simplicity, the cramping of their short lines. The less literal of the two also tries to approximate the absolute regularity of their meter, which (supplemented by the rhyme) does to the poem's language what the calm that the language evokes does to the sea. This is language that affords utterance no change, no motion that is not a kind of stillness.

First as to sense:

Deep stillness rules the water,
Without motion rests the sea,
And in anguish sees the sailor
Level surface all around.
No breeze from any side!
Death-stillness dreadful!

In the monstrous breadth
Moves not one wave.

Then as to sound:

Deep in stillness stands the water
With no motion rests the sea
And in anguish sees the sailor
Level surface like a lea.
Not a breath from any quarter!
Deathly stillness eerily!
In the monstrous breadth of water
Moves no wave the eye can see.

Tiefe Stille herrscht im Wasser,
Ohne Regung ruht das Meer,
Und bekümmert sieht der Schiffer
Glatte Fläche ringsumher.
Keine Luft von keiner Seite!
Todesstille fürchterlich!
In der ungeheuern Weite
Reget keine Welle sich.[1]

Even read silently, the poem speaks, but its speech is turned against itself. Unable to be silent, the poem conveys the feeling of being harried by silence, of having speech invaded by the silence everywhere around it. The language is pinched, minimal, clenched; the words are unable to make progress, condemned to make the same observation over and over. The exclamations in the third couplet momentarily cancel the very ability to make a statement, to utter a full sentence. The second exclamation, with its wrenching inverted word order, pinpoints exactly what this ubiquitous silence and its toll on language communicate: it is death. The word *Todesstille*—dead calm—means exactly what it says.

Music too can evoke the effects of a silence that it breaks in the act of depiction. Schubert's song "Meeresstille" does so by constricting its piano accompaniment in much the way that Goethe constricts his poem's language. The accompaniment consists of an unvaried series of slow arpeggios (chords played one note at a time). It is less a form of motion than an audible cancellation of the rich variety of motion normally available to

Example 1. Schubert, "Meeres Stille" (Calm Sea).

Meeres Stille

music. It is motion as monotony. And on Schubert's piano, even with the pedal engaged, each arpeggio would have died away to silence before the next one began. But even more than by its sound, the song portrays dead calm by the way it *looks*. Even for those who do not read music, the score (example 1) creates a vivid image of emptiness, motionlessness, and sound muffled, even strangled. The fixed columns of whole notes spread out wide to form a surface on which the voice floats in a narrow, mostly low compass, as if the vocal line were becalmed within the staff.

7 Prisons of Silence

Dead calm at sea has a landlocked equivalent. Both Goethe's "Calm Sea" and Schubert's musical setting of it take the becalmed sea as a kind of prison. In onshore life in the early nineteenth century, some prisons fashioned themselves into becalmed seas set in stone.

The most notorious of these was Eastern State Penitentiary in Philadelphia, which became a tourist attraction within a few years of its opening and remains one today; it ceased housing prisoners in 1970. Eastern State was America's first penitentiary. From its opening in 1829 until nearly the end of the century it held all of its inmates in solitary confinement. (This policy was officially revoked in 1913 but had broken down under its own weight years earlier.) The prisoners lived and worked under a regime of enforced silence. No visitors were allowed. All communication was forbidden; the prohibition was enforced not only by the guards but also by unusually thick cell walls. The system and the structure were designed, on Quaker principles, to elicit penance—hence the name *penitentiary*. What they elicited instead was torment.

Charles Dickens visited Eastern State on his tour of the United States in 1842 and subsequently published an account of the cruelties of its system of punishment. The forced silence struck him as one of its worst offenses. Like the calm sea of Goethe and Schubert discussed in the previous entry, the silent prison reduced those caught in it to a condition of death in life:

Standing at the central point, and looking down [the] dreary passages, the dull repose and quiet that prevails, is awful. Occasionally, there is a drowsy sound from some lone weaver's shuttle, or shoemaker's last, but it is stifled by the thick walls and heavy dungeon-door, and only serves to make the general stillness more profound. Over the head and face of every prisoner who comes into this melancholy house, a black hood is drawn; and in this dark shroud, an emblem of the curtain dropped between him and the living world, he is led to the cell from which he never again comes forth, until his whole term of imprisonment has expired. He never hears of wife and children; home or friends; the life or death of any single creature. He sees the prison-officers, but with that exception he never looks upon a human countenance, or hears a human voice. He is a man buried alive.[1]

The silence that Dickens found in America took hold in Britain later in the century. The most outspoken of its critics was Oscar Wilde, who experienced "the silent system" firsthand during his own imprisonment between 1895 and 1897. In a letter published after his release, Wilde lambasted the "stupid and barbarous" system that left prisoners "deprived of books, of all human intercourse, isolated from every humane and humanizing influence, [and] condemned to eternal silence."[2] In the poem he wrote about his prison experience, "The Ballad of Reading Gaol," he observes a detail that epitomizes the whole prison regime. The prison guards wore felt-soled shoes so as not to disturb the dead silence. In their creeping and peeping and furtive tread, they seem more criminal than the prisoners do:

> The warders with their shoes of felt
>   Crept by each padlocked door,
> And peeped and saw, with eyes of awe,
>   Grey figures on the floor.[3]

The twentieth century reformed these abuses in some places but revived them in others. The officials in charge of the Russian gulag grasped the imprisoning power of dead silence very well. In her book *Silence*, which also deals with Eastern State, Jane Brox quotes the educator and journalist Eugenia Ginzburg (1904–1977) on the Russian variety. Ginzburg spent eighteen years as a political prisoner in the gulag. Her account emphasizes the *physical* injury imposed by unbroken silence, which spreads through the body like a malignancy: "The silence thickened, became tangible and stifling. Depression attacked not only the mind but the whole body. Even my hair seemed to bristle with despair. I would have given anything to have heard just one sound."[4]

8 Just One Sound

It would have given Ginzburg her world back. For Jean-Jacques Rousseau, it could take away the weight of the world.

In his *Reveries of a Solitary Walker*, Rousseau recalls seeking happiness in "the simple feeling of existence" and nothing more:

> If there is a state where the soul can find a resting-place secure enough to establish itself and concentrate its entire being there, with no need to remember the past or reach into the future, where time is nothing to it, where the present runs on indefinitely but this duration goes unnoticed, with no sign of the passing of time, and no other feeling of deprivation or enjoyment, pleasure or pain, desire or fear than the simple feeling of exist- ence, a feeling that fills our soul entirely, as long as this state lasts, we can call ourselves happy, not with a poor, incomplete, and relative happiness such as we find in the pleasures of life, but with a sufficient, complete and perfect happiness which leaves no emptiness to be filled in the soul.[1]

But this resting place for the soul needed a resting place for the body, which Rousseau found in nature. In particular he found it in places of repose where embodiment felt bodiless, first in a gently rocking boat on a lake and then by the bank of a murmuring stream. In *The Hum of the World* I observed that this simple feeling of existence—the sensation of being—did not exclude external sensation but actually rested on it. But not just any external sensation. The rocking motion seems obviously maternal, consist- ent with Rousseau's own account of himself in his *Confessions* as one who forever sought to replace the mother he lost in infancy. The sound of the stream forms a lullaby. (Rousseau's notorious badness as a father—he insisted that all his children by Thérèse Levasseur, as many as five, be aban- doned at foundling hospitals—might intimate a desire to be the one and only child, the only son.) But the account of Rousseau's search concludes with what you have just read, the lulling sound, the murmur, of a flow of speech that says nothing but itself. The happiness that Rousseau pursues might be criticized as mere self-absorption but it is more like self-surrender. It feels like the apprehension of self but not of ego. Its rest is absolute because it asks for nothing, and asking for nothing is what it is. But it is possible only with a material support, which it finds in the sound of moving water at the threshold of audibility. Its rest depends on the hum of the world.

Commenting on Rousseau's description, Simon Critchley focuses on the experience of what might be called time at rest. Rousseau describes a time that (like a murmuring stream) seems to flow but not to pass, as if the relationship of past to future had been suspended. One knows it is there but does not sense its workings. Critchley says of this state that it is "to be in time with no concern for time."[2] He goes on to describe his own experience of this knowing unconcern, which also leaves bodily motion behind and leads to the sound of water. And he writes the sound; note the alliterative rhythm of *s* words from *sleep* through *surf* and the half rhyme of *held* and *lulled:*

> [One can] sit by the sea in fair weather or foul and feel time disappear into tide, into the endless pendulum of the tidal chronometer. At moments like this one can sink into deep reverie, a motionlessness that is not sleep, but where one is somehow held by the sound of the surf, lulled by the tidal movement.[3]

The sound that Critchley hears does not measure time passing but time persisting: "a time older than the time of chronometers." The tidal chronometer is a chronometer of timelessness, a chronometer of the audible. The last quoted phrase is not from Critchley but from T. S. Eliot, who in "The Dry Salvages" describes

> The tolling bell [that]
> Measures time not our time, rung by the unhurried
> Ground swell, a time
> Older than the time of chronometers, older
> Than time counted by anxious worried women
> Lying awake, calculating the future . . .
> Between midnight and dawn, when the past is all deception,
> The future futureless, before the morning watch
> When time stops and time is never ending;

And the ground swell, that is and was from the beginning,
Clangs
The bell.[4]

Eliot offers a salutary reminder that what was bliss for Rousseau and Critchley two centuries apart may also be terror. The endlessness of sounding time may just as well be an abyss as a caress. The terror sounds on, not so much in the percussive clang of the bell (echoed in the clash of consonants in *clang*) as in the resonance it leaves behind. The after-clang fills the pause imposed between the last two lines by the white space they leave on the page.

9 Song and Sound

In his *Essay on the Origin of Languages* (1754), Rousseau links the communicative power of language to certain elemental properties of sound. In the course of doing so, he inevitably encounters music, and he welcomes the encounter: "As soon as vocal signs strike your ear, they herald a being like you. . . . Birds whistle, man alone sings, and one can hear neither song nor symphony without immediately saying to oneself, another sentient being is here."[1] Many of us would nowadays be inclined to decline Rousseau's distinction and say that birdsong is as much a mark of sentience as human singing, but his underlying idea remains intact: song requires sentience; therefore we hear sentience when we hear song. Singing makes sentience discernible. And if this is right, we might even go further and say that sentience requires song. To communicate itself directly to the senses of another, the sentient being must sing. When the "vocal sign" strikes the ear in song, it ceases to be a sign and becomes a vibratory presence. Song gives sentience a sensory medium.

But if song is sentience, sound is something more. As I put it in *The Hum of the World,* sound is the measure of life. But life, as opposed to living beings, is not sentient in itself, so the parallel between sound and song is inexact. For most living beings capable of the act, to declare oneself alive means to make oneself heard. Being seen is not enough; the visual is the realm of illusion as much as it is the domain of truth. In the first scene of Shakespeare's *Hamlet*, which is all about making oneself heard, the watchman Marcellus expresses his frustration that Hamlet's friend Horatio will not believe that the watch has twice seen the ghost of Hamlet's father. The only remedy, which will prove that the ghost is real, and thus in some sense still imbued with a vestige of life, is speech:

> Horatio says 'tis but our fantasy
> And will not let belief take hold of him
> Touching this dreaded sight twice seen of us.
> Therefore I have entreated him along
> With us to watch the minutes of this night,
> That, if again this apparition come,
> He may approve our eyes and speak to it.[2]

The aim of the spiritualism craze that gripped the English-speaking world from the mid-nineteenth century through the 1930s was not to see spirits but to speak with them. The mediums, to be sure, did tricks with "ectoplasm" and the original version of smoke and mirrors, but the crowning act of the séance was the sound of the spirits speaking through the medium's voice. William Butler Yeats's 1934 play *The Words Upon the Window Pane* takes the sound of the spirits, many of whom do not know they are dead, as a central theme. "A state of somnambulism and voices coming through [the medium's] lips that purport to be those of dead persons?" asks one character incredulously. "Exactly," replies another.[3]

The climax of the play says so too. It takes the form of an extended argument between the spirits of Jonathan Swift and the lover he named "Vanessa" (Esther Vanhomrigh). The quarrel interrupts the séance, which had no interest in Swift despite being held in a house he once had visited. The spirits of Swift and Vanessa take control of the medium against her will and relive their troubled relationship in the medium's mouth.

A more metaphorical scene of returning to life through sound—and a happier one, though not untroubled—comes at the beginning of part 2 of Goethe's *Faust* (1830). Recovering from the tragedy recounted in part 1, Faust lies sleepless in a pastoral valley attended by the Ariel of Shakespeare's *The Tempest*. Ariel is a spirit known best for his enchanting songs. But although he does have his attendant spirits sing to Faust, the latter's revival occurs in association with a cosmic sound not previously heard of, let alone heard. The sound is the rumble of sunrise—a "tremendous roar":

> Hearken! How the hours near!
> Thundering in the spirit's ear
> Now the newborn day appears.
> Rocky portals open chattering,
> Phoebus' wheels go rolling, clattering,
> What a roar the daylight's bringing!
> Its trumpets, its trombones are sounded,
> Eyes are blinded, ears astounded,
> The unheard-of stays unheard.
> Slip into a flower bell,
> Deeper, deeper, there to dwell,
> In the rocks, beneath a leaf:
> If it strikes you, you'll go deaf.[4]

The life-giving sunrise comes not with lyrical dawn sounds or birdsong but with a tone of frightening power—reminiscent of the long, slow crescendo that evokes the world's first sunrise in Haydn's oratorio *The Creation* (1798): an ascent through ten consecutive whole notes over gathering instrumental forces, culminating in a *fortissimo* cadence with drum strokes till then (in this number) unheard of. Goethe simply reverses the direction. Instead of building up from essentials, he builds down to them. His passage from song to sound is a descent from sentience to the raw stuff of life. That stuff turns out to be auditory, vibratory. The eye is blinded ("Auge blinzt": it blinks against the glare) but the ear is astounded; its sensory power is raised, not lowered. Although the result is a reawakening, a return to life, there is real menace in the enigmatic line "The unheard-of stays unheard" ("Unerhörtes hört sich nicht") and in the power of the sublime sound to strike the hearer deaf. The flower bell is a refuge as well as a womb.

10   Already Music

Accounts of perceiving the hum of the world—what I call the *audiable*—go back to classical times. When Virgil's Aeneas visits the underworld, the assembly of souls waiting to be reborn brings to mind a scene of pastoral bliss. The blessed shades crisscross the Elysian Fields

> just as, in the meadows, on a cloudless summer's day,
> the bees settle on the multifarious flowers, and stream
> round the bright lilies, and all the fields hum with their buzzing.[1]

Essential to this description, but easy to forget, is the realization that there are no bees in Elysium. Instead the streaming of the shades emits a pleasing background hum that, like the sound of bees in earth's summer meadows, permeates the fields of asphodel.

But when does the audiable become perceptible in music?

In 1801 Samuel Taylor Coleridge echoed Virgil in a poem entitled "Inscription for a Fountain on a Heath." The inscription begins by addressing an overhanging sycamore tree "oft musical with bees!" and ends by inviting the passing pilgrim to refresh his spirit "listening to some gentle sound, / O[f] passing gale or hum of murmuring bees." In between, the inscription voices an auditory wish:

> Long may the Spring,
> Quietly as a sleeping infant's breath,
> Send up cold waters to the traveler
> With soft and even pulse!

Before the fountain refreshes the traveler's body by quenching his thirst, it refreshes his spirit by the motion of its "soft and even pulse." The fountain's pulse embodies the pulse of life. And even more than a motion, this pulse is a sound, issued by the spring "quietly as a sleeping infant's breath"—the breath of life continually renewed at its point of origin. This quiet sound hovers on the threshold of perception, and from there it predicts its own unbroken continuation. The fountain refreshes not only with its cold clear waters but also with the sound that it mingles with the audiable. As the water flows, so flows the sound.

Virgil implicitly and Coleridge explicitly hear that sound as already a kind of music, which raises a further question. It is a question of great interest to me since my scholarly work is mainly involved with music—Western classical music to be exact—and I am also a composer. How can the audiable be expressed musically? Is there a way for music to reveal somehow its own foundation in, or its own emergence from, the universal background of all sound? If so, when did the audiable become audible in music?

It is impossible to locate a first time. Virtually everything has a precedent, and in any case the audiable probably entered music in the experience of performances that have left no record. But it is possible to locate an iconic instance, a symbolic rather than actual first that left its mark on most subsequent realizations of the audiable in music. That instance—is this any surprise?—occurs at the beginning of Beethoven's Ninth Symphony.

One of the most remarkable things about this celebrated passage is how short it is: just ten measures of *pianissimo* for strings and horns, plus solo clarinet (from m. 5) and solo oboe (mm. 9–11) before a crescendo begins that will have swept up the whole orchestra to *fortissimo* at the end of m. 16 (example 2).

The underlying conception of musical sound, or music as sound, is double. First, the music forms a kind of origin myth. It exemplifies the faint, diffuse sonority from which melody and harmony emerge. The passage has no melody of its own, just a scattered falling figure in two notes, the bare minimum, all open fourths and fifths. The harmony, on the dominant, is hollow and static, consisting wholly of empty fifths—chords with a note missing. That void quickly becomes audible in its own right and assumes an intensifying feeling of potentiality. The sounding gap becomes the root of the audiable that grounds and permeates the soft persistence of the other sounds—sustained wind tones (horns and clarinet are capable of playing very quietly) and shimmering tremolo strings, disturbed only by those falling figures (which are marked *sotto voce* in the first violins).

The second part of the conception is carried by the brevity of the passage; those first ten measures are over before we can fully grasp them. Their potentiality reveals itself and is realized and then drops below the threshold of audibility as the sounds of the orchestra pile up. The symphony thus begins with a gain—of a cadence, a melody, a sonorous fullness—that is also a loss. For that reason, perhaps, the gain is imperfect. The cadence is violent, the melody harsh and angular, the sonority a top-to-bottom unison. It is as if the music has not been patient enough, as if it had not listened carefully enough. The seventy minutes or so that remain

Example 2. Beethoven, Ninth Symphony, first movement, mm. 1–16.

Symphony No. 9

I

Example 2. (continued)

are devoted to finding a remedy, a task that ultimately passes to the voices added for the concluding "Ode to Joy."

11   Coming Alive

In his *Rhetoric*, Aristotle invented a word, *energeia*, to designate a concept that he may have invented along with it: the effect produced by an orator whose language is so vivid that it seems to bring to life what it describes, as if to put an action before the listener's eyes. The idea has had a long history under various names—vividness, lifelikeness, verisimilitude—and its link to visualization has remained intact, though at the cost of observing that enargeia actually emerges in the transition between real sound, in the orator's voice, and imaginary sight. The vividness comes not just from the language, with its metaphors and other devices, but also from the utterance of the language. The language is potentially vivid; the utterance makes it actually so. This dependency makes it all the more striking that from classical times on, the quest for energeia has migrated freely from speech to writing. If the writing is read silently, which was probably a regular practice by late antiquity, the need for sound would seem to disappear.[1]

But it does no such thing. To achieve energeia, to come alive for the reader, writing needs sound no less than speech does. It must find ways to incorporate sound in its nominally silent sphere. The need is parallel to what proved, historically, to be a basic need of cinema—the need to animate the moving image, not just with music, but with a soundtrack, not just with voices, but with ambient sound. This need was not unique to the medium of film. Instead, film's moving images turned out to be the exemplary case of the need for sound to create the impression of life. When mute moving images on screen first became technologically possible, they fell into what we nowadays call the uncanny valley, the discomfiting zone where the too-human and the not-quite-human overlap. In its need for sound, silent cinema exposed the more general need for sound as the medium of animation and thus brought out the fundamental relationship between sound and the sensation of life.

That relationship becomes pivotal for writing when writing moves beyond its purely practical uses—those it was invented for—to the uses of culture. Once it becomes more than record keeping, writing becomes discomfited by its formerly neutral muteness; or rather the muteness becomes evident and troubling precisely when writing begins to describe, narrate, and express. Hence writing develops the need to seem lifelike, which it does by seeming sound-like.

To that end writing begins to borrow from auditory sources external to it, though in ways that are impossible to put into a neat chronological sequence. Writing incorporates meter, phonetic play, rhythmic repetition, and rhetorical figures of speech, the last in the original sense of the term referring to manner of statement as opposed to figures of thought such as metaphor. Figures of speech arose in part as memory aids, but in part to enable an orator to put body (originally *his* body, a gender preference that still has repercussions today) into the act of utterance, to reinforce tone with posture and gesture. The bodily element carries over into writing as a potential for utterance that is diverted into the space of silent reading via the reader's body or bodily memory. The carryover is strong enough that the reading experience is not really silent even though no sounds are uttered. *The Hum of the World* explores this condition under the rubric of the "half-heard."

But the auditory manner of expressive writing also seeks to extend itself into the matter, as if manner alone did not go far enough or get close enough to meaning, or substance, or experience. Metaphor rings out; the figure of thought also becomes a figure of—that is, a figure for—speech. One key result is the interpolation of auditory descriptions into the written text. These are usually passages that interrupt a narrative (as passages of visual description may also do) or that extend a reflection or observation. They are usually passages that reflect on and explicate the semblance of life that arises in sound. These passages have not customarily received much critical attention, but they deserve to have the omission rectified.

One famous example occurs early in William Wordsworth's poem "Ode: Intimations of Immortality." The poem begins by lamenting the loss of a "celestial gleam" that the young Wordsworth used to see everywhere in the world but that the elder, who speaks in the poem, can no longer see. But the speaker's first impulse is to seek relief in sound, not sight. And he seeks

not one sound, but many, a ringing sphere of sound that is nearly violent
in its intensity:

> Now, while the Birds thus sing a joyous song,
>   And while the young Lambs bound
>   As to the tabor's sound,
> To me alone there came a thought of grief;
> A timely utterance gave that thought relief.
>   And I again am strong.
> The Cataracts blow their trumpets from the steep:
> No more shall grief of mine the season wrong:
> I hear the Echoes through the mountains throng,
>   The winds come to me from the fields of sleep,
>   And all the earth is gay;
>   Land and sea
>   Give themselves up to jollity,
>   And with the heart of May
>   Doth every Beast keep holiday;—
>   Thou Child of Joy,
> Shout round me, let me hear thy shouts, thou happy Shepherd Boy!

At first Wordsworth measures his feeling of revival by his receptivity to
sound, sounds filling the distance to reach his ears. But the more he hears,
the less confident he feels: he must hear more, and more again, and he can
never hear enough. By the end of the passage, two big changes have occurred.
Wordsworth's assertion that he hears the joyous sounds around him has
become a plea to hear those very sounds. And the affiliation between life and
hearing turns around into the affiliation of life with being heard. By the end
of the passage, the text is mimicking the shouting that it calls for—and that
it fails to hear except in its own raised voice. The shouting reaches the reader
in the medium, the genuinely auditory medium, of the half-heard.

12 The Vocal Telegraph

Herman Melville's first book, *Typee* (1846) is a fictionalized memoir of his
experience in the South Pacific. Melville had taken a job as an able seaman

on a whaling ship, but, finding the voyage mismanaged by a tyrannical captain, he jumped ship on the island of Nuku Hiva, part of the Marquesas chain, and spent a month in the valley of Taipivai (the "Typee" of the title, which also names the inhabitants) in 1842. At one point he describes a "vocal telegraph" used by the Typee to carry messages across a distance, but the description in the novel's two published versions is sketchy. But the unpublished manuscript draft is vivid: "These sounds at first scarcely audible & advancing progressively from the water's edge swelling higher & higher as they approached their maximum at the place where I stood, & then sweeping still on & sinking away by an inverse gradation until they became lost again to the ear, suggested to me the idea of a gamut whose notes were sounded by a giant."[1]

Melville here inverts a comparison common in his day that presented the sound of the telegraph as a kind of speech. The telegraph key in particular bore frequent comparison to a tongue. But the key clattered; if it spoke, its voice was made entirely of consonants. Melville adds the vowels. His elaboration of the trope of the talking telegraph softens the sound of the device, reclaiming the mechanical for the organic. The change suits the place of this long-distance relay of voices in what the narrator perceived (at the time) to be a tropical paradise uncorrupted by modernity. The mechanical telegraph carried further than voices could, but it did not carry so well.

The sound of the vocal telegraph becomes transformed as it moves across the land. The linked voices adopt the wave motion of the sea from which the relay starts, ebbing and flowing in a pattern of crescendo and decrescendo that also transforms the sound into a kind of music. The explicitly musical image of a gamut played by a giant extends the musical metaphor to mythic proportions. A gamut—the full pitch range of a musical instrument—large enough to be played by a giant would suggest the compass of the whole island, if not the whole world. The vocal telegraph resounds with the full harmony of nature. In doing so it unites nature with culture—represented by the communal voice—in a manner no longer available in the "civilized" world.

Earlier in the published text, the auditory foundation of this primordial singing telegram becomes perceptible in the alienated sound of the narrator's own voice: "As we advanced through this wilderness, our voices sounded strangely in our ears, as though human accents had never before disturbed the fearful silence of the place, interrupted only by the low murmurings of distant waterfalls."[2] The silence is fearful because the only thing keeping it from being total is scarcely present: the barely audible low murmurings of the distant waterfalls. In nature those murmurings would be continuous, so their interruption of the silence must be understood to occur not in the material wilderness but in the ear of the narrator. The sound is easy to lose track of. The ear must search for it to break the silence, and the silence must be broken by listening rather than by speaking because the sound of the narrator's voice is too estranged to defend him against the fearfulness.

13 The Ravished Ear

The seventeenth-century Flemish singer and composer Leonora Duarte (1610–ca. 1678) was accustomed to holding musical evenings with her family in Antwerp; the whole family was musical. Duarte apparently had a beautiful singing voice. We know, at least, that her singing moved one visitor, the English poet-philosopher-playwright Margaret Cavendish, to something like ecstasy: "[Her voice] Invites and Draws the Soul from all other Parts of the Body, with all the loving and Amorous Passions, to sit in the Hollow Cavern of the Ear, as in a Vaulted Room, wherein it Listens with Delight and is Ravished with Admiration."[1]

The metaphors in this statement are complex, and Cavendish's seventeenth-century punctuation is ambiguous. The images carry more weight than the assertion. But the probable logic of the sentence follows from the fact that it specifies only one listener in the cavern of the ear. In all likelihood, Cavendish is saying that Duarte's voice employs or arouses the amorous passions in order to draw the soul, which is ordinarily diffused throughout the sensitive body, into a single tight-knit form seated in the ear. For Cavendish, Duarte's singing offered an intrinsic auditory epiphany—a *coup d'oreille* (see entry 3). The voice is ravishing and the listener is ravished.

From a vocal perspective, Cavendish's remark is revealing because of its suggestion that the effect of pure voice is to annul the other senses so that only the ear is active. Pure voice puts one in a hollow cavern that itself forms a gigantic ear. Life and sentience concentrate in listening and heed nothing else. The result, however, is double: Cavendish's listener receives delight, suggesting the act of giving aesthetic consent, but she also undergoes ravishment, suggesting a passive, helpless surrender to amorous passion. The force of the moment comes from the meeting of these opposites in the attentive and receptive ear.

The image of the cavern also recalls the cave of the nymphs in Homer's *Odyssey*, where bees hum and two springs perpetually flow and from which the battered and weary Odysseus will be symbolically reborn. The passage from the *Odyssey*, in the sixteenth-century translation by George Chapman that Cavendish would have known, is more alert to auditory sensations than Homer's original:

> There is a port,
> That th' aged sea-God Phorcys makes his fort,
> Whose earth the Ithacensian people own,
> In which two rocks inaccessible are grown
> Far forth into the sea, whose each strength binds
> The boist'rous waves in from the high-flown winds
> On both the out-parts so, that all within
> The well-built ships, that once their harbour win
> In his calm bosom, without anchor rest,
> Safe, and unstirr'd. From forth the haven's high crest
> Branch the well-brawn'd arms of an olive-tree;
> Beneath which runs a cave from all sun free,
> Cool, and delightsome, sacred to th' access
> Of Nymphs whose surnames are the Naiadés;
> In which flew humming bees, in which lay thrown
> Stone cups, stone vessels, sh[u]ttles all of stone,
> With which the Nymphs their purple mantles wove,
> In whose contexture art and wonder strove;
> In which pure springs perpetually ran;
> To which two entries were; the one for man,
> On which the North breath'd; th' other for the Gods,
> On which the South; and that bore no abodes
> For earthy men, but only deathless feet
> Had there free way.[2]

From the wider auditory perspective of *The Hum of the World*, the most revealing element in Cavendish's description is the vaulted room.

The image suggests a church filled with choral song—in Chapman's terms a vault of art to strive with the cave of wonder. The vaulted room situates Duarte's voice in a space meant to amplify sound, to diffuse reverberation, echo, and resonance. The space invokes the tingling presence of the audiable, which the voice fills out as it fills the space up. Goethe once said that architecture is frozen music. Some centuries earlier, Cavendish implies that music is melted architecture.

14 Campaniles

On a day in July in 2019 I was fortunate enough to be seated with my wife on a shaded outdoor terrace overlooking the city of Florence not far from the dome of the great cathedral. It was a Sunday, and as noon struck the church bells began to sound from all directions around the city. They did not all sound at once, however, but pealed in a kind of complex antiphony and polyphony—antiphony because one set of bells often answered another, their distinctive timbres and pitch levels engaging in a resonant dialogue, and polyphony because two, three, or even four sets of bells at times sounded simultaneously. As we listened the air filled not only with the individual tones of the ringing bells, but also with the sum of their resonances, which was as much palpable as it was audible and which carried the ringing like an auditory surface spread out on all sides, a realization of the hum of the world—the audiable. The sense of the hum became especially pronounced as the last of the bell sounds faded away, solo, like a final cadence. For a brief moment, the air seemed to tingle with the remnant of the ringing, now felt more than heard and yet faintly audible as well, as the bell tones previously carried by the audiable merged into it, momentarily bringing the hum to the surface of audibility even as they sank beneath the same surface. After another moment the sounds of ordinary life resumed, unperturbed, but enriched, while we sat there, by a passing tranquility with no object other than itself.

Sometime around 1877, Nietzsche had a similar if more troubled experience:

In Genoa at the time of evening twilight I heard coming from a tower a long peal of bells: it seemed it would never stop, resounding as though it could never have enough of itself over the noise of the streets out into the evening sky and the sea breeze, so chilling and at the same time so childlike, so melancholy. Then I recalled the words of Plato and suddenly they spoke to my heart: nothing human is worthy of being taken very seriously; nonetheless—[1]

Which prevails, the self-perpetuating, self-pleasing bell sounds diffusing into the audiable or the melancholy chill that denigrates human life? The chill is real enough, but, as Nietzsche says, resoundingly, singling out and striking the one word like a bell: *trotzdem,* nonetheless—

15 Cannonades

The thirteen-hundred-year narrative of Edward Gibbon's *The Decline and Fall of the Roman Empire* ends with the capture of Constantinople by the Ottoman Turks in 1453. Gibbon is very precise about the date: "the memorable twenty-ninth of May, in the fourteen hundred and fifty-third year of the Christian Era." He also gives a vivid description of the assault, but he cuts it short to say that no adequate description is possible—the first time he has done so in a book full of battle scenes. He rejects the heroic style of epic for the sobriety of the historian:

> The single combats of the heroes of history or fable amuse our fancy and engage our affections. . . . But in the uniform and odious pictures of a general assault, all is blood, and horror, and confusion; nor shall I strive, at the distance of three centuries, and a thousand miles, to delineate a scene of which there could be no spectators, and of which the actors themselves were incapable of forming any just or adequate idea.[1]

Instead of continuing to describe what happened, Gibbon tells us how the assault on the city *sounded.* The distance of three centuries and a thousand miles does not stand in the way of his account. He almost seems to understand the fall of the city as primarily an auditory event. The Turkish galleys approach the city walls:

Under pain of death, silence was enjoined: but the physical laws of motion and sound are not obedient to discipline or fear; each individual might suppress his voice and measure his footsteps; but the march and labor of thousands must inevitably produce a strange confusion of dissonant clamors, which reached the ears of the watchmen of the towers.[2]

Gibbon can be sure of the dissonant clamors because they are based on physical laws; the approach of the galleys could have sounded no other way, and their sound was the sound of doom. The same logic rules the account, later in the same long paragraph, of the moment the empire fell. The voice of the emperor Constantine XI is heard encouraging his soldiers but is drowned out by the tumult. The sultan Mehmet II, wielding a mace in the air, all but calls down thunderbolts to strike the walls:

The tide of battle was directed and impelled by his voice and eye. . . . The cries of fear and of pain were drowned in the martial music of drums, trumpets, and atabals [Moorish kettledrums]; and experience has proved, that the mechanical operation of sounds, by quickening the circulation of the blood and spirits, will act on the human machine more forcibly than the eloquence of reason and honor. From the lines, the galleys, and the bridge, the Ottoman artillery thundered on all sides; and the camp and city, the Greeks and the Turks, were involved in a cloud of smoke which could only be dispelled by the final deliverance or destruction of the Roman Empire.[3]

The sound of the weaponry becomes a monstrous music; the sound of the martial music becomes a weapon. The cacophony of warfare attacks the body no less forcibly than shot and shell. When the battle hangs in the balance, and with it the fate of the empire, its uproar decides the outcome. For Gibbon, the Roman Empire literally falls with a bang.

16   Soundless Hearing

English has no word in common use to form an auditory parallel to *visualization* and its cousin *envision*. Descriptive writing, especially in literature, assumes that whatever is described may be seen in the mind's eye of the reader. Note that I do not use scare quotes around *seen*. When I read a

description and visualize what I read, the act of seeing is more than meta-
phorical; the mental images form an actual presence, though not a mate-
rial one. But descriptions of sound cannot be received in the same way. A
scene described becomes visual but sounds described remain verbal.
Musicians, it is true, may be able to hear what they read (or write) in a
score, but that is a special skill. The capacity to visualize is assumed to be
universal.[1]

There would seem to be only one way to overcome this limitation, and
that is to hear the effect of the sound described on the language that
describes it. The text does not have to be read aloud for this to happen; the
language of the text also has a sound when read silently. This sound is
perceived but not heard, as a mental image is seen but not eyed. Such half-
heard sound, as I have called it, has the potential to become the substance
of, for lack of a better term, an audiolization. And like visualization, audi-
olization does not depend on a prior reality. One can perceive sounds that
have never been heard just as one can see scenes that have never been
eyed. The boundary between the sensory and the mental, always fluid, is
especially so with nonacoustic sound and nonocular sight.

The most overt literary examples of audiolization are imitative. They
occur when the rhythmic and phonetic qualities of a text become echoes
of the sounds that the text refers to, even, to stress the point, if those
sounds are purely fictional, as they most often are. These sounds have
never been made except in the acts of reading that mimic them. Famous
or notorious poetic examples include Edgar Allan Poe's "The Bells" (1849)
and, a century or so earlier, Alexander Pope's self-referential illustration of
verbal mimicry in his "Essay on Criticism," with its dictum that "the sound
must seem the echo to the sense":

> To the tintinnabulation that so musically wells
> From the bells, bells, bells, bells,
> Bells, bells, bells—
> From the jingling and the tinkling of the bells.
>
> *(Poe)*

> Soft is the strain when Zephyr gently blows,
> And the smooth stream in smoother numbers flows;
> But when loud surges lash the sounding shore,

The hoarse, rough verse should like the torrent roar,
When Ajax strives some rock's vast weight to throw,
The line too labors, and the words move slow;
Not so, when swift Camilla scours the plain,
Flies o'er the unbending corn, and skims along the main.

(Pope)

(And yes, I am making a phonetic play on "Poe" and "Pope." The implication of continuity is a transparent illusion, an author's trick that Pope would recognize: the sound must *seem* an echo to the sense. But this author's trick includes one little touch of reality, since Poe is so clearly following Pope's sonorous injunction about sonority and even invents the word "tintinnabulation" to help himself out. How could I do otherwise?)

The verbal imitation of nonverbal sound has a wide range, from the blatant to the subliminal. But the effect of imaginary sound on the half-heard text is not limited to imitation. Auditory description is no less capable than its more familiar visual counterpart of shaping the mood and meaning of a text. This fact is only remarkable because it has not been more remarked on. It has been underappreciated despite the evident care that texts have long taken with their sonority. One reason for this neglect is the general and age-old bias toward vision as a model of knowledge. But another reason—and also something not sufficiently remarked on—is the peculiar independence of the meaning of words from their sound. This independence is limited; there are many occasions on which what a statement means depends on how it is uttered; Pope's "seem" is a good example. But it is nonetheless true that one can understand the majority of sentences, at least roughly, no matter what they sound like. The aim of the sonorous text is to revoke the semantic privilege of the unspoken word. The text can be fully understood only if it is well heard.

Take, for instance, the opening stanza of "Atlantis," the final poem in Hart Crane's *The Bridge*. The instance is particularly revealing because what the stanza describes, the Brooklyn Bridge, is *seen* as a kind of music. The suspension cables become both the staves of a score and the strings of a lyre:

Through the bound cable strands, the arching path
Upward, veering with light, the flight of strings,—

Taut miles of shuttling moonlight syncopate
The whispered rush, telepathy of wires.
Up the index of night, granite and steel—
Transparent meshes—fleckless the gleaming staves—
Sibylline voices flicker, waveringly stream
As though a god were issue of the strings.[2]

The bridge here, played on by moonlight, becomes a material embodiment of divine harmony. Its only actual sound is a "whispered rush," the faint sound of the wind in its cable strands, which act as a wind harp, but that is enough to release "Sibylline voices," the voices of those through whom the god Apollo speaks. So it is not music but rather the god himself that sounds or, more, issues, comes into being, through the flight of strings. It is the music that makes the god divine, not the other way around.

In saying all this, however, I have not yet broken the independence of the words from their sounds. But the stanza is clearly asking its reader to do just that: to hear it better. Its harmony is not a premise but a goal, the "arching path" to which is half-heard sound. The poem's utterance begins as a jumble, with sentences and phrases in uncertain relation to each other, their harmony inchoate. The music described by the stanza must issue from the verse the way the god issues from the strings. The poetry must do more than bear witness to the music of the bridge; it must sing that music into existence.

The first hint of this creative primacy comes in the lines "Taut miles of shuttling music syncopate / The whispered rush, telepathy of wires." The underlying pulse of the stanza, as of the poem, is blank verse, iambic pentameter. But the line about the taut miles performs the syncopation that it refers to, beginning with the spondee "taut miles" and continuing with the inability of the last syllable of "syncopate" to bear a strong stress. The missing stress rushes the ensuing enjambment to the "whispered rush." This auditory jolt has real consequences. As if shaken, the ensuing three lines fall out of the metrical order and into grammatical obscurity. It remains for the last line of the poem to restore the harmony that it claims has been present all along. And this it does by stating the desired outcome in the only perfect iambic pentameter line in the stanza, the concluding line: "As though a god were issue of the strings." The firm ending on "strings" rectifies the wavering movement of "syncopate." Only by "audiolizing" the stanza in its half-heard form can the silent reader understand fully what has been read.

Although my examples here have come from poetry, there are innumerable instances of prose that would have done as well. The difference between poetry and prose in this context is that poetry takes as a necessity what prose takes as a possibility. The underlying issue, however, belongs neither to poetry nor prose but to language, the sound of which is so all-pervasive that we have not chosen often enough to listen to it closely.

"Words live in the mind." So said Virginia Woolf in the only surviving recording of her voice, broadcast on BBC radio in 1937.[3] The phrase becomes a refrain as Woolf speaks, sounding a little different each time she says it. Its recurrences gradually build up to the question of just *how* words live in the mind, and in the mind alone. The answer is that they live there as half-heard sound, or the readiness to become so. Words can never be severed from their origins in speech: "[They] are full of echoes, of memories, of associations. They have been out and about, on people's lips, in their houses, in the streets, in the fields, for so many centuries." Woolf proves the point by adapting a line from a sea shanty, "The Maid of Amsterdam," the rhythmic sway of which recalls, half heard, the melody that goes with them. The choice of shanty may seem odd for Woolf, because the words complain about the sexual treachery of women:

> I'll go no more a-rovin' with you fair maid
> A-roving, A-roving, since roving's been my ru-i-in
> I'll go no more a-roving with you fair maid.[4]

Woolf picks up the rhythm and identifies the English language with the Victorian stereotype of the loose woman, the siren or femme fatale who breaks all the rules of conduct, class, nationality, and race:

> And how do [words] live in the mind? Variously and strangely, much as human beings live, by ranging hither and thither, by falling in love, and mating together. It is true that they are much less bound by ceremony and convention than we are. Royal words mate with commoners. English words marry French words, German words, Indian words, Negro words, if they have a fancy. Indeed, the less we enquire into the past of our dear Mother English the better it will be for that lady's reputation. For she has gone a-roving, a-roving fair maid.[5]

Words happily acquire this bad character because they are "the wildest, freest, most irresponsible, most un-teachable of all things." They echo, however faintly, a roving cry of sexual pleasure. Their sound takes us to places where their sense would get in the way.

17   The Talking Dead

In April 1889 Robert Browning made a voice recording on an Edison cylinder. For some reason the cylinder was kept under lock and key until December 12, 1890, the first anniversary of Browning's death. On that day members of the London Browning Society held a commemorative observance, in this case more like a séance, in which Browning's recorded voice made its public debut. The image of a séance is not mine; it comes from H. R. Haweis's description of the "extraordinary séance" in the *London Times:*

> This is the first time that Robert Browning's or any other voice has been heard from beyond the grave. It was generally known that Colonel Gouraud had got locked up in his safe some words spoken by the poet . . . at the house of Rudolph Lehmann, the artist. But up to yesterday the wax cylinder containing the record had never been made to yield up its secret. . . . The small white wax cylinder containing the record carefully wrapped in wool was produced, and, on being put upon the machine, the voices at Rudolph Lehmann's house on the night of April 7, 1889, were accurately reproduced. . . . While in breathless silence the little, awed group stood round the phonograph, Robert Browning's familiar and cheery voice suddenly exclaimed: "Ready?"[1]

There was nothing acoustically unusual about the contents of this recording. Though still novel, voice recording had already become familiar; people were used to it. What they were *not* used to was the realization of a power inherent in the technology: the phonograph could make the dead speak.

That power was the reason for Haweis's image of a séance, which, however, falls short in one respect: unlike the ventriloquisms of a medium, the sound of Browning's voice could be *verifiably* resurrected. The description in the *Times* suggests an exhumation more than it does a séance. The voice has its own coffin in the "small white wax cylinder" that, extracted from its secret place in Colonel Gouraud's safe, can be "opened" by the phonograph to reveal the voice made audible in death as it was in life. The voice was real, and really Browning's. It sounded familiar and, speaking from the past, announced its own return in the present, repeatable at any present time: "Ready?"

The resulting feeling of amazement did not last long. People quickly got used to the voices of the dead. The phonograph, and later sound film and its audiovisual offspring, would fill the world with them, and even with the talking dead themselves. We tend to think nothing of this; it is the stuff of everyday life. But for a brief moment in history the speech of the dead produced awe and wonder. For that reason, Haweis's description suggests a religious ceremony even more than it does a séance. The wax cylinder, carefully wrapped in wool, is the housing of a saint's relic even more than it is a coffin.

But not everyone heard things this way. A notable exception was Browning's sister, Sarianna, who wrote to a friend in outrage: "Poor Robert's dead voice to be made interesting amusement! God forgive them all. I find it difficult."[2] For the grieving sister, Browning's voice is dead, and, what's more, it should *stay* dead. To bring it back is a kind of sacrilege that Sarianna cannot, in truth, forgive. Underlying this protest is another inherent power, this one belonging to voice, not to the machine. Voice always sounds alive. Machine voices, which have existed since the eighteenth century, sound mechanical, although digital voice technology promises, or threatens, to change that. But when we recognize a sound as someone's voice, the voice sounds alive. The members of the Browning society were not discomposed by the poor signal-to-noise ratio of the cylinder recordings, and neither was Sarianna Browning. For the devotees, the recorded voice was too alive to die; for Sarianna, it was too alive for comfort.

This small historical episode helps reveal a basic asymmetry in the archival possibilities of auditory and visual media. The cultural West has long been invested in images of the dead; few people have had difficulty with them. All portraiture, whether sculpted, painted, or photographed, has a mortuary element; a good part of its value rests with the power to preserve the appearance of the portrait's subject, especially the appearance of the face. Only in the nineteenth century does the portrait as a literary trope take on sinister implications, from Edgar Allan Poe's "The Oval Portrait" to Oscar Wilde's *The Picture of Dorian Gray*. But this is also the era in which both portrait painting and portrait photography flourished on a vast scale. One reason for this dual development is the increasing realization, perhaps powered by photography, that even images that resemble their originals "to the life" are themselves removed from life. They are not "dead" exactly, especially not after the images learn to move, but they are palpably nonliving. Life, we might surmise, cannot commemorate itself; it must be commemorated from outside.

Recorded voice has none of these qualities. Its lifelikeness proliferates throughout any medium capable of reproducing it. Although we know it is not alive, we cannot help hearing a kind of life in it. Its nonliving dimension is present but rendered inoperative. If the recording medium transmits more noise than signal, the medium sounds mechanical but the voice holds onto a kernel of vitality, as if refusing to die into the mechanism of its reproduction. The only way to kill a recorded voice is to make it inaudible. The proximity of sound to life, which I trace in detail in *The Hum of the World*, persists to some degree in all recorded sound. But voice is its superlative degree.

18 From Sounds to Sound

We travel to see the sights, but not, it seems, to hear the sounds. When a sight attracts our gaze, we talk about it as something worth seeing, or something one must see, or an unforgettable sight. The scenes we seek out for enjoyment present themselves as forms that reward our seeing, but not, as a rule, as forms of sight. With sounds almost the opposite happens. Almost, because, as so often with seeing and hearing, the difference is an asymmetry, not an opposition. The sounds we hear with pleasure, even including music, present themselves both as forms that reward listening and as forms of sound. Sight, paradoxically, tends to disappear into what is seen. Sound makes itself heard in addition to what we hear. I can always hear sound when I hear a sound, but to see sight when I see a sight requires further reflection. That happens when, for example, a painting or photograph or film represents the gaze that takes it in. But the appeal of sound precedes its representation: the appeal is in the peal.

When we attend to sound as sound, the audiable comes within the range of our hearing. We may not hear it directly—that remains rare—but we can hear it reverberating in the way that the sounds we do hear combine and reinforce each other. As sound envelops what is sounded, the hum of the world becomes its overtone as well as its undertone.

This peculiar vibrancy extends to literary descriptions of sound, insofar as the descriptions seek to add their own auditory value to the value of the sounds they describe. This addition cannot be reduced to mimicry, though mimicry may be a part of it. The sounds we hear or half hear in the text become responses to the call of the absent or fictitious sounds that the text records.

For example, consider a stanza from one of the most popular British poets of the early nineteenth century, until recently almost wholly forgotten: Felicia Hemans (1793–1835). The reasons for Hemans's long eclipse are complex; suffice it to say for now that her lyrical gifts were too often at odds with an earnest moralizing strain that the twentieth century in particular found hard to stomach. Hemans also had a morbid preoccupation with death that lacked the bizarre gusto of her American near contemporary Edgar Allan Poe. But Hemans was also preoccupied with sound. There is perhaps more auditory imagery in her poetry than in any comparable body of work. The present example comes from a long lyric, "Easter-Day in a Mountain Churchyard":

> And lo! where, floating through a glory, sings
> The lark, alone amidst a crystal sky!
> Lo! where the darkness of his buoyant wings,
> Against a soft and rosy cloud on high,
>   Trembles with melody!
> While the far-echoing solitudes rejoice
> To the rich laugh of music in that voice.

Two auditory features of these lines stand out, at least to my ear. One is the sense of a sound that bursts into prominence by breaking through a barrier that appears only when it is broken. The barriers are visual, and pleasant: a glory, or halo of sunlight, amid which the lark floats, and the roseate cloud against which the bird's dark wings beat, and, beating, become a form of melody. In each case a sight becomes a form of sound that pleases in itself. The language of the stanza parallels this break-through in two ways. There is the closely spaced repetition of "Lo!," advancing from the second syllable of line 1 to the first syllable of line 3; the enhanced repetition translates the injunction to look into an occasion of listening, carried by a long and strong vocalic sound. And there is the lurch between lines 1 and 2, "sings / The lark"; sharply curtailed at both ends, enjambment straightforwardly identifies the lark's song with a wel-come rupture, or rapture.

The indented line, "Trembles with melody," is imitative; it consists of two dactyls, that is, groupings of three syllables in the pattern DUM-ti-dum. Compressed and set apart, the line too trembles, and with the poem's melody. But the two concluding lines, a closed couplet, have greater con-ceptual weight. The key factors here are the spondees (adjacent strong syllables) in the first half of each line: "far-echoing" and "rich laugh." By slowing the movement of the verse, these verbal nubs bring out the need to linger over the sound of the lark's song as it extends in depth and breadth to the far-echoing solitudes. The reader, though, has access to only one far-echoing solitude, made up of the stanzas set apart on the page to emulate the sound they describe. Only by becoming absorbed in their half-heard chant, only by reading along with it, can the reader as listener share, if at all, in the pleasure and knowledge borne on the lark's song.

These intimations are not purely aesthetic in a narrow sense. In a poem about Easter, the rising of the lark and the need to linger over its song have a transparently religious force. Hemans's lark, acoustically and otherwise, echoes both Shelley's skylark, "That from Heaven, or near it, / Pour[s its] full heart / In profuse strains of unpremeditated art" ("To a Skylark") and Shakespeare's, which "at break of day arising / From sullen earth, sings hymns at heaven's gate" (Sonnet 29). Shakespeare and Shelley make their larks' songs heavenly but take heaven as a metaphor for the beauty of the sound that falls to earth. Hemans does the reverse. She invokes the sound as the medium in which the flight of the lark embodies the literal act and promise of ascent to heaven.

19   Fictitious Sounds

Whenever I watch a film based on a familiar novel, I find myself faintly disappointed in the look of both the places and the people. It does not matter whether the film is done well or poorly. It does not even matter if the fictitious place is real. In the 1985 film version of E. M. Forster's *A Room with a View* (a film I quite like), even the river Arno (a river I like even more) looks a little wrong, as if it were impersonating itself. There is a sense in which fictionalized scenes and selves can never be made fully visible. The fact of fiction, so to speak, always intrudes. Something similar occurs—for me, anyway—with photographs, which seem to make visible things and people I have never seen, but to veil a little the people and things I have seen.

Sound is not troubled in the same way. Fictitious sounds—voices or music or soundscapes described in language—cannot be heard acoustically, but they are perceptible nevertheless in the medium of the half-heard, the virtual sound of the language that describes them. This happens best when the language is minimally or indirectly imitative rather than overtly onomatopoetic. The perception of fictitious sound is most lifelike when, as noted in the previous entry, the sound of the language registers as a response to the sounds that in one sense have merely been imagined (the very term is visual), but in another, more important, sense have been summoned by the language that describes them into a kind of sensory half being.

As to sound in films, which is nearly always the product of editing as well as recording, the strange thing is that it tends to seem real no matter what form it takes, perhaps because the sound is not an image of something else but an actual, present sonority. Even a sound that represents another sound, like that of a flute or piano imitating birdsong, is sonorously real. An image cannot be continuous with a thing; a sound cannot be otherwise. We all know we can't believe what we see, but we know too that what we hear is what we hear (even if we also know better). With sound, and especially with music, the fact of fiction blurs into auditory presence. If I listen, say, to a piece from Olivier Messiaen's *Catalogue of Birds* for piano, I know perfectly well that I am not hearing a bird, or rather I don't need to know it; the issue does not come up. But at the same time I *am* hearing something I might also hear in a bird's song: a resonance, a fluctuation, a sound resounding.

Here, once again, we encounter an asymmetry between sight and sound that is not inherently an opposition. Words and images and sounds can all refer, but words and images (always both partners and antagonists) can refer only at a distance. Sounds refer immediately, traveling, however tenuously, across their distance from their acoustic referents. Words may be fictitious, images are always fictitious, but there is no such thing as a fictitious sound.

One consequence of recognizing these differences is the collapse of the idea that sound stands outside of sense and symbolization and belongs with the substrate of reality that no representation can capture. This recognition fosters the further realization that there is no such substrate. There is no X that looms like dark matter or an abyss of the unknowable beneath the intelligible world. To think otherwise is to commit a classic error of the kind that Wittgenstein sought to expose in the *Philosophical Investigations,* very much a book in which the evocation of sound, intonation, and emphasis is part of the argument. The fact that something always escapes my representation does not mean that there is *a* something that escapes. What eludes representation is just as fluid and variable as representation itself. This fluidity, moreover, is not a defect, except in reference to an impossible ideal of certainty. It is the condition of possibility of thinking, knowing, and imagining. The change in status that recognizing this condition brings to sound is important, not because it elevates sound—though it elevates our awareness of it—but because it widens the scope of our entire sensory and conceptual world.

20 Bells

"What passing bells for those who die as cattle?" asks Wilfred Owen in his famous poem "Anthem for Doomed Youth." Like most of his work, the poem was spurred by World War I; Owen would be killed a week before the fighting ended. His answer is that there are no such bells, nothing like the bells that, for example, Tennyson invoked in his "Ode on the Death of the Duke of Wellington":

> Let the bell be toll'd,
> And a reverent people behold
> The towering car, the sable steeds.
> Bright let it be with its blazon'd deeds,
> Dark in its funeral fold.
> Let the bell be toll'd,
> And a deeper knell in the heart be knoll'd;
> And the sound of the sorrowing anthem roll'd
> Thro' the dome of the golden cross.

Tennyson makes sure that the reader can hear the passing bell sounding in his verses, as rhymes to "toll'd" proliferate across lines of varying length. Owen does the same thing—but with the sounds that replace, which here means supplant, the sound of the bells:

> — Only the monstrous anger of the guns.
>   Only the stuttering rifles' rapid rattle
> Can patter out their hasty orisons.

Owen's reduction of the peal of the bell to a stutter, and prayer to a patter, drowns out the sound of reverence and national sentiment that Tennyson, writing as poet laureate, called on with such sublime confidence in 1852—the very confidence that, in its blindness, doomed the youth of Owen's generation in 1914.

But why, apart from its role in funerals, the sound of the bell? Why, in other words, did the bell acquire the role of which Owen strips it?

One answer may lie in the sensory ambiguity of bell sounds, which make audible the latent association between sound and mortality.

Sound, especially in the era before sound recording, is perceived only in its vanishing and, once gone, it is gone for good. The sound of a bell draws that process out, makes the vanishing slow down so that the ear can trace its course and detect the failure of the senses to retain what they perceive. Hence the bell tolls, and as John Donne famously wrote, it tolls for thee. Yet at the same time, quite literally *in* the same time, the sound of the bell intimates that something may linger, may be held yet a moment longer, may even return in or from the medium into which it passes.

The nineteenth-century lyric was very absorbed in this dimension of sound and often sought to imitate it, not only with bell sounds but with echoes, refrains, and the summoning of voice—invocation. Here is a simple but not atypical instance, the first of the two stanzas of Felicia Hemans's "Oh, ye Voices Gone":

Oh!, ye voices gone,
  Sounds of other years!
Hush that haunting tone,
  Melt me not to tears!
All around forget,
  All who loved you well,
Yet, sweet voices, yet
  O'er my soul ye swell.[1]

The text is troubled by the sense that the voices that are gone are not gone at all, and that to hear them still is too sad to bear. But in the very act of lamenting the persistence of the lost voices the poem brings their sounds back, contradicting its own stated wishes: every line five syllables long, mostly monosyllabic, all the lines metrically identical, and all but the penultimate line end-stopped, which gives auditory form to the swell that, in both word and act, closes the stanza. But the topic of the lyric does not have to be sound for the sound of the lyric to carry the paradox forward— to toll or to peal like a bell:

Swallow, my sister, O singing swallow,
  I know not how thou hast heart to sing.
    Hast thou the heart? is it all past over?
Thy lord the summer is good to follow,

> And fair the feet of thy lover the spring:
>   But what wilt thou say to the spring thy lover?
>
> O swallow, sister, O fleeting swallow,
>   My heart in me is a molten ember
>   And over my head the waves have met.
> But thou wouldst tarry or I would follow,
>   Could I forget or thou remember,
>   Couldst thou remember and I forget.

The first of these stanzas from Swinburne's "Italys" invokes singing. The second does not, but the verbal melody of the two is just the same. One refrain of the swallow echoes the other, as all the refrains do throughout the poem, as does the echoing wordplay throughout. The repeated chant makes sound audible. The incantation rings like a bell, persistently subsiding into the "molten ember" from which it takes wing again like an auditory phoenix.

21 Dis/Embodiment

When does recorded voice become disembodied? In audio and audiovisual media alike the answer is simple—and the same. Voice becomes disembodied when we do not know whose voice it is. In audiovisual media, that happens with voice-off narration by an unidentified narrator. We do not always have to see who is speaking, but we do have to *know* who. In audio media, disembodiment has no distinctive venue, no equivalent to the voice-off. The same recording will sound embodied if we know the source of the voice and disembodied if we do not.

What is remarkable about audio-only embodiment is that so little is required to establish it. All one needs is a name. Just the name makes the body audible, along with a measure, large or small, of context and history. The more the name means, the more embodied the voice sounds. The name, moreover, does not merely correct a disembodiment inherent to voice recording. On the contrary, it changes the conditions of perception so that the *embodiment* inherent to voice recording becomes apparent.

For that reason, the famous people who in the 1890s recorded their voices on Edison cylinders often took care (or were coached) to name themselves—in effect, to add their acoustic signature to the sound of their voice. The need to impress oneself, so to speak, on the cylinder is particularly clear in a recording that includes the voice of Brahms. The composer at first identifies himself as "Doctor Brahms" in soft, almost hesitant, tones, but immediately, as if sensing that his presence was too hazy, he reaffirms it viscerally with an emphatic "Johannes Brahms!"[1]

In Arthur Conan Doyle's "The Story of the Japanned Box" (1889), an alcoholic widower keeps himself sober by secretly playing his wife's dying words to himself on a phonograph, the japanned box of the title. The recorded voice is realistic in a double sense: it sounds just like the woman who made the recording, and it reveals the condition of her body with perfect clarity. "Yes," says the narrator, "it was a woman's voice; there could not be a doubt of it. But a voice so charged with entreaty and with yearning love, that it will ring for ever in my ears. It came with a curious faraway tinkle, but every word was clear, though faint—very faint, for they were the last words of a dying woman."[2] The revelation that the voice is recorded is the climax and close of the story, which is framed as a kind of mystery. Prior to that revelation, however, everyone who overhears the voice from outside is convinced that there is really a woman in the room.

The same logic applied to tenors, or at least to one in particular. Marketing recordings by its operatic superstar, Enrico Caruso, the Victor Talking Machine Company trumpeted the reality of his recorded voice. In one ad from 1913, a photographed Caruso stands dressed for one of his signature roles, Rhadames in Verdi's *Aida*. Next to him is a large image of a phonograph disk, which appears over the boldface caption "Both are Caruso" (figure 1). The text under the caption embroiders the theme: "The Victor Record of Caruso's voice is just as truly Caruso as Caruso himself. It actually *is* Caruso. . . . [Y]ou hear him [in your own home] just as truly as if you were listening to him in the Metropolitan Opera House." The singer's photograph, running the full length of the full-page ad, commends the power of the recorded voice to retain the impress of the body that produced it.[3]

Figure 1. Victor Company ad, "Both are Caruso" (1915).

22 Threads

John Banville's novel *Snow,* published in 2020, turns on a murder in an Irish country house—a dilapidated grand estate that one of the characters describes as Edgar Allan Poe's House of Usher. The lady of the house, a dead ringer for Madeline Usher, has already made an entry and exit like Madeline's in Poe's tale. Subsequently, the detective inspector sent to investigate the crime, trudging along a lonely road, meets another fugitive from Poe: "A hunched crow, perched on a high branch, eyed him as he went past and opened wide its black beak and cawed at him."[1]

A little earlier the inspector takes a phone call from his chief: "When there was a lapse . . . on the line, if Strafford listened hard he could hear, behind the electronic crackles, a sort of distant warbling. It always fascinated him, this eerie, cacophonous music, and gave him a shiver too. It was as if the hosts of the dead were singing to him out of the ether."[2] Eerie though it may be, this notice from the audiable that yes, it is still there, it is always there if you listen hard enough, is a kind of lifeline—pun intended—in a world where death, remote from the ether, admits no singing. The muteness of that world is embodied in the snow of the novel's title, which adds a layer of literary resonance to go along with the allusions to Poe. The snow, of which it is said repeatedly that more is coming, recalls the famous concluding paragraph of James Joyce's "The Dead." At one point Strafford quotes from it: "Snow was general all over Ireland." Joyce goes on: "It was falling on every part of the dark central plain, on the treeless hills, falling softly upon the Bog of Allen and, farther westward, softly falling into the dark mutinous Shannon waves. It was falling, too, upon every part of the lonely churchyard on the hill. . . . It lay thickly drifted on the crooked crosses and headstones, on the spears of the little gate, on the barren thorns."[3]

The soft snow muffles all sound but the faint sound of its falling. Its fall affects the mind as much as the ear: "It seemed to Strafford the snow was falling not only on the world but in his head, too. It might go on falling forever, stealthily, silently, muffling all sound, all movement."[4] All? Perhaps not quite. The warble on the phone line cannot be muffled; it makes audible the sound that remains when all other sound has been subtracted. Its auditory line is the thread that leads out of the labyrinth of snow. Strafford's tragedy is that he has lost the thread.

23 Playback

In 1861, sixteen years before the invention of the Edison phonograph, a device on which he would subsequently record part of "The Charge of the

Light Brigade," Alfred Tennyson twice transformed nature itself into a phonograph—first in person, then in a poem. Rather than form a medium of memory, the natural scene became a medium of sound recording, doing what, until 1877, was literally impossible: playing back the sound of a departed voice. In doing so it drew on one of the most evocative powers by which the audiable makes itself audible to the receptive ear: the power of one sound to modulate into another, to make the experience of listening a change in the aspect presented by an otherwise continuous flow of sound.

Tennyson's experience occurred in the Pyrenees, in the place for which he named the poem, "In the Valley of Cauteretz":

All along the valley, stream that flashest white,
Deepening thy voice with the deepening of the night,
All along the valley, where thy waters flow,
I walked with one I loved two and thirty years ago.
All along the valley, while I walked today,
The two and thirty years were a mist that rolls away;
For all along the valley, down thy rocky bed,
Thy living voice to me was as the voice of the dead,
And all along the valley, by rock and cave and tree,
The voice of the dead was a living voice to me.

Tennyson took the walk he recalls here with his friend Arthur Henry Hallam, whose early death became the occasion for his, Tennyson's, extended elegy—133 lyrics long—*In Memoriam*. Revisiting the scene, Tennyson addresses the stream, the "voice" of which he had heard deepening all the previous night—deepening, as if to reflow into the sound of a man's voice. The voice that the stream plays back is, like the stream itself, unbroken, and hence unspeaking; as streams do, it murmurs. It is not the speech that comes back but the tone, the timbre, the quality that makes the voice recognizable for whose it is. And for Tennyson, there is no doubt: what he hears is not *like* Hallam's voice; it *is* Hallam's voice, modified only by its recording medium— as all recorded voices would be a few years later. The text marks this certainty when it changes from the mode of as-if ("Thy living voice to me was as the voice of the dead") to the mode of unqualified predication ("The voice of the dead was a living voice to me"). With that avowal, the poem ends.

Or not quite: because the poem also records its own sound, becoming a kind of verbal valley full of echoes meant to carry over beyond the act of reading, preeminently the fivefold "All along the valley." The phrase begins every other line with its fluid vowel sounds, tracing its path on the air as if on the curve of the Edison cylinder looming just over the horizon, the only boundary to the flow of the voice-stream.

24 Shorthand

In "Art as Technique," written in 1917, the Russian critic Viktor Shklovsky introduced the concept of defamiliarization, the art of making the familiar seem strange, or, better yet, of retrieving the original strangeness of all things. Defamiliarization, also translated as "estrangement," restored the luster to perceptions tarnished by use:

> Habituation devours work, clothes, furniture, one's wife, and the fear of war. "If the whole complex lives of many people go on unconsciously, then such lives are as if they had never been" [Tolstoy]. And art exists that one may recover the sensation of life; it exists to make one feel things, to make the stone stony.[1]

It's an attractive idea, and one that carries a measure of truth. But (apart from the fact that art does many other things as well) it is too confident in the power of art to cancel habituation, which is not so easy; habituation may really be irreversible. Which is why, to recover or uncover knowledge about, for example, how sound changed in the era of sound recording, together with what formerly unremarked things the fresh experience of recorded sound revealed about sound in general, it makes sense to study recorded sound in the historical moment before it became second nature.

One of those revelations concerns the strange romance between signal and noise. A retrospect on this topic appears in the 2005 poem "Phonograph," by Sandy Florian.[2] The title plays on the fact that the term "phonograph," which since the mid-twentieth century has referred almost exclusively to record players, historically had several other meanings. One of them, the technique of shorthand invented by Isaac Pitman in 1837, is the fulcrum on which the poem turns. Florian takes shorthand as the epitome of writing itself, and hence of her text itself; all writing, she suggests, captures the sound of a voice, but only in abbreviated form. Like a phonograph record, which reproduces what the sound of a voice *was,* writing preserves not only a voice but also the loss of that voice. At the same time, Florian composes the text in a manner that mimics the noise of the needle in the phonograph groove, especially the sound of the pops and clicks that occur when the groove is damaged. She isolates transitional words, punctuating with periods between them, as if she were taking dictation and writing down even the speaker's pauses and hesitations. Although she uses the technique in other contexts, in this one it seems to reproduce its own origins:

> I say, Perfect. I say, Yet. This instrument warbles. And. This record is warped. And. The tongue of this snake. Has scratched this disk. For. Your voice is skipping. And. As I put the conch to my same hear, I listen to the echo of. I listen to the echo of. The raspy susurrations of your adieu.

Florian begins her poem with an allusion to Pitman shorthand and later refers to "Pitman's phonograph"; in between she also writes the enigmatic sentence "The old man's laugh comes to us as out of a phonograph." If we follow the clue in that line, it leads us to a historical meeting between Pitman's phonograph and Edison's, which turns out to be a story about signal and noise.

The *London Daily News* for October 20, 1891, carried a story announcing the first meeting of the Phonographic Society—which is not what it sounds like. The Phonographic Society was formed to promote Pitman shorthand. According to the paper, though, one good phonograph deserved another. Both were devices of prosthetic speech: "The speech of Sir Isaac Pitman, who is unable to attend personally, will be delivered by the [Edison] phonograph, a special messenger having been dispatched by Colonel Gouraud to Bath for the purpose of recording it."[3]

As an earlier entry has recounted, Gouraud was the Edison Company's representative in England, and the man who secreted away a recording of Robert Browning's voice to be unveiled at an 1890 meeting of the London Browning Society commemorating the first anniversary of the poet's death. Pitman's absence was less absolute, though he was in his eighties at the time. On October 22, the *Aberdeen Free Press* reported that the two ingenious inventions for mastering the human voice were brought in contact tonight at the annual meeting of the London District of the Phonographic Society. Mr Isaac Pitman was unable to be present in the flesh, yet his spoken message was entrusted in Bath yesterday to Edison's phonograph, and was delivered tonight in London to his disciples. Before the phonograph delivered Mr. Pitman's speech, Colonel Gouraud explained [that] . . . Pitman, knowing that his remarks were to be uttered in a large hall, had attempted to raise his voice in proportion, with the result that his speech came in a somewhat vague and husky manner from the phonograph. Nevertheless, it could be heard by an attentive listener at the back of the building. The diplomas of the Phonographic Society were afterwards distributed, and there was an exhibition of typewriting, which is becoming a vast industry for young women in the Metropolis.

The correspondent for the *Coventry Evening Telegraph* heard things differently. He was even more impressed than his colleague by the alliance between "the two ingenious inventions for mastering the human voice":

Phonography and the phonograph were in pleasant companionship last night. The occasion was the first annual meeting of the National Phonographic Society—an association founded to advance a well-known system of shorthand writing. . . . The venerable founder—Mr. Isaac Pitman—was unable to be present, but the speech that he would have delivered was spoken by him at Bath on the previous day, and recorded by one of Edison's phonographs. By this means it was reproduced with such clearness that every word was heard by the audience which filled the Memorial Hall, London.

The two newspaper articles unintentionally anticipate the ambiguity that increasingly haunts recorded sound as technology improves: noise, like the groove noise on a phonograph, interferes with the signal, but it must also be accepted as precisely the element that validates the signal. In the early years of recorded sound, the sheer fact of the recording fostered a high tolerance for noise, at times bordering on deafness to it; greater fidelity made noise more audible and thus less tolerable. In this perennial antiphony, the long-playing vinyl record may have represented a golden mean. At least it became, or has become in retrospect, the exemplary case. It reveals that while noise puts gaps in the signal it also fills the signal with spectral presences that would otherwise go unheard, unsensed. The imperfection of the groove is the imperfection of life. Perfection is mummification.

25 Poems to Music

The title phrase of this entry does not refer to poems *set* to music, but to the much rarer phenomenon of poems *addressed* to music. Rarer still are poems addressed to a specific composition, poems that take a piece of music in all its particularity as a kind of interlocutor, almost as another person.

Two poems by Thomas Hardy, who was an avid music lover, fit this description especially well. One, "Apostrophe to an Old Psalm Tune," marks Hardy's lifelong fascination with a melody that changes as he encounters it over the years. The other, "Lines to a Movement in Mozart's E-Flat Symphony," addresses itself to music that does not seem to change in the hearing, but that undergoes a metamorphosis in the sound of Hardy's verse. Both poems make themselves into music, not, as convention would dictate, by making themselves mellifluous, but instead by modeling themselves after the sound to which they speak. Each address forms half of a polyphonic whole, best heard if the poem is read—chanted—aloud. Hardy made no voice recordings, though he lived until 1928, and the language of his verse is often gnarly, notoriously so. But elocution was a prominent concern in the Victorian age, and recordings of poetry from the early twentieth century suggest that a chanting intonation would be more or less expected. It is certainly apparent in the recordings made by William Butler Yeats of his iconic "The Lake Isle of Innisfree": Yeats virtually sings the first line, "I will arise and go now, and go to Innisfree." (His voice captures the way the line seems to sing itself around its central moment of transient silence.)

"Apostrophe" is dated Sunday, August 13, 1916. Attending church that day, "in these turmoiled times of belligerent fire," Hardy unexpectedly meets a long-lost friend—the psalm tune of the title. Apostrophe, normally an address to an abstraction or to a person absent or dead, here becomes an intimate address, as if spoken face to face. But it also reads as if sung tune to tune. The first line, "I met you first—oh, when did I first meet you?," combines conversational language with the verbal music of chiasmus, as the second half of the line intones the first half in reverse. The last stanza clothes the tune and gives it a face while also telling us, in the present tense, how the poet matches his intonation to the music's, and how the reader should, too: "So, your quired oracles beat till they make me tremble / As I discern your mien in the old attire." Hardy has had a history with this tune, but he has not heard it in a long time. Its "living on" amid the fires of the Great War awakens the hope that it may also live "onward" beyond them.

The poem is designed to hold on to that hope by forming a music of its own that corresponds to but does not imitate the sound of the tune. (We have no idea what tune it is or how its melody goes.) Like many of Hardy's poems, "Apostrophe" invents a unique stanza form that becomes its acoustic signature. Each of its seven stanzas is five lines long, rhyming *abbcc*. The first three lines contain ten or more syllables, most with four stresses; the fourth line contains five to seven syllables, most with three stresses; the fifth line contains five or six syllables, always fewer than the line preceding it, most with two stresses. Thus the full first stanza:

I met you first—ah, when did I first meet you?
When I was full of wonder, and innocent,
Standing meek-eyed with those of choric bent,
While dimming day grew dimmer
In the pulpit-glimmer.[1]

Tune to tune, the series of seven stanzas corresponds to the strophic repetition of the psalm's "quired oracles." The poem renders each strophe, in sound, as an act of concentration, a paring down of utterance to an essential core that embodies, but does not identify, the source of the tune's fascination.

"Lines to a Movement in Mozart's E-Flat Symphony" also uses a five-line stanza based on the expansion and contraction of the number of syllables in each line. In this case there is a gradual extension in lines 1–3, a wide leap in line 4, and a sharp contraction in line 5, which carries the refrain, repeated without variation in each of the four stanzas. The stanzas are also linked by cross-stanza rhyming, uniform in the third lines, and forming a chiasmus across the fourth lines, *abba:*

> Show me again the time
> When in the Junetide's prime
> We flew by meads and mountains northerly! –
> Yea, to such freshness, fairness, fulness, fineness, freeness,
> Love lures life on.
>
> Show me again the day
> When from the sandy bay
> We looked together upon the pestered sea! –
> Yea, to such surging, swaying, sighing, swelling, shrinking,
> Love lures life on.
>
> Show me again the hour
> When by the pinnacled tower
> We eyed each other and feared futurity! –
> Yea, to such bodings, broodings, beatings, blanchings, blessings,
> Love lures life on.
>
> Show me again just this:
> The moment of that kiss
> Away from the prancing folk, by the strawberry-tree!
> – Yea, to such rashness, ratheness, rareness, ripeness, richness,
> Love lures life on.[2]

Here again, the verbal music arises from the unique sonority of the stanzaic pattern rather than from any imitation of the music, which, like the psalm tune, remains unknown. Hardy does not say which movement the poem is addressing, nor even which E-flat symphony, though the likeliest candidate is no. 39, the first in the sequence of three famous symphonies that Mozart wrote in 1788. The slow movement of no. 39 does contain music that the poem may be seeking to pair with, especially since pairing is the main theme of the poem.

Hardy asks the music to revive four long-ago moments of romantic intimacy, or, if we take him at his word, to show them again as present, not to the eye but to the ear. Each time he asks he affirms—wants to affirm—that in such moments "love lures life on." The affirmation, the fourfold "yea," sits uneasily by the word "lures," which implies deception, disappointment, and disillusionment. What Hardy asks the music to bring back is, so to speak, the allure of the lure. The auditory form of that return arises in the fourth lines, with their alliterative sequence of five ardent two-syllable words, separated by commas, each with the same suffix (-*ness* or -*ing*). The sound has the same "beating" quality that Hardy hears in the recovered psalm tune, the same beating, striking, trembling, throbbing, pulsing by which love or music lures life on.

Mozart, it so happens, composed that beating into the slow movement of his Symphony no. 39. The movement features a recurrent passage in which the strings repeat a succession of detached two-note figures moving gradually from the upper register to the bass. Most of these figures pulse between rests that go by like quick breaths. Their motion resembles a cascade of two-syllable words throbbing and beating as they well up, sink a little, hover, then sink steadily away. It is not much of a stretch to describe them in words of like pulse drawn from Hardy's poem: "surging, swaying, sighing, swelling, shrinking." It is impossible to know for sure if Hardy had this passage in mind, but he and Mozart are surely, almost literally, on the same wavelength.

26 Grooves

In Richard Flanagan's 2013 novel *The Narrow Road to the Deep North*, set during World War II, the incipience of an illicit affair is marked by the reluctance of the parties involved to break an embrace and say goodbye. Their reluctance is echoed by the sound of a phonograph needle repeating in the empty groove at the center of the record—the sound of an ended song. The needle, we read, "was ch-ch-ing as it circled the record's end." And a moment later: "The needle remained stuck in the groove, scratching circles of sand into the night."[1] Those circles of sand will prove several kinds of portent; the affair will happen, but we already know things will not end well. The music that has ended, a popular ballad about lost love, has already told us that: "These foolish things / Remind me of you." The needle's lingering records the lovers' inability to separate, but it also exposes the void that will inexorably open up beneath them.

The scene of the needle in the groove is only the most recent in a series that perhaps begins with Aldous Huxley's novel *Point Counter Point*, from 1928. The music in this case is not a popular song but the slow movement of Beethoven's String Quartet No. 15 in A Minor, op. 132. The movement carries a title that reads, in English translation, "Sacred Song of Thanks to the Godhead from a Convalescent, in the Lydian Mode":

> Spandrell was very insistent that they should come without delay. The *Heilige Dankgesang eines Genesenen an die Gottheit, in der lydischen Tonart* simply must be heard. "You can't understand anything until you have heard it," he declared. "It proves all kinds of things—God, the soul, goodness—unescapably. . . . You *must* come."
>
> "Most willingly," said Rampion, "But . . ."
>
> Spandrell interrupted him. "I heard quite by accident yesterday that the A minor Quartet had been recorded for the gramophone. I rushed out and bought a machine and the records specially for you."
>
> [Spandrell] wound up the clockwork; the disc revolved; he lowered the needle of the sound box onto its grooved surface. A single violin gave out a long note, then another a sixth above, dropped to the fifth (while the second violin began where the first had started), then leapt to the octave, and hung there suspended through two long beats.
>
> More than a hundred years before Beethoven, stone deaf, had heard the imaginary music of stringed instruments expressing his inmost thoughts and feelings. He had made signs with ink on ruled paper. A century later four Hungarians had reproduced from the printed reproduction of Beethoven's scribbles that music which Beethoven had never heard except in his imagination. Spiral grooves on a surface of shellac remembered their playing. The artificial memory revolved, a needle travelled in its grooves, and through a faint scratching and roaring that mimicked the noise of Beethoven's own deafness, the audible symbols of Beethoven's convictions and emotions quivered into the air . . . long notes, a chord repeated, protracted, bright and pure, hanging, floating, effortlessly soaring on and on. And then suddenly there was no more music; only the scratching of the needle on the revolving disk.[2]

Like its successor in *The Narrow Road*, the groove noise in this passage is irreducibly ambivalent. On the one hand it represents lifeless mechanism, the void beneath the music, the very condition from which the convalescent of the *Heilige Dankgesang* has been spared. The dismayed observation of the "scratching of the needle on the revolving disk" corresponds to the realization that being spared the void is always only temporary, in this case a respite that lasts exactly as long as the recording does—or, as it turns out, a little less. On the other hand, the grooves of the record provide the medium that conveys the music to the listener. The grooves even possess a kind of sentience since they remember the playing of the music. They even recall the noise of the deafness that Beethoven had overcome in writing his score, another kind of phonographic recording. The scratching sound is simultaneously a portent of death—a death that will end this scene, when Spandrell is murdered—and an expression of mourning.

The condition that Robert Pfaller named "interpassivity" is fully at work here: the machine both remembers for us and laments for us.[3] The mechanism takes the place of the subjectivity that employs it. Interpassivity, however, may occur outside our experience: we record the broadcast that we never watch. But in this case the assumption of subjective agency by the machine is vicarious: we can *hear* it substituting for us. And we continue to hear it as the scratching needle goes on both to signify and to protest another kind of death, the social death meted out by the proto-Fascist regime that hunts Spandrell down.

The experience of a respite that lasts only as long as a recording does, also under the cloud of Fascism, returns in Virginia Woolf's final novel, *Between the Acts*. Written in 1939, the book was published shortly after Woolf's suicide in 1941 when the skies of London were roiling with the Blitz. Its groove noises are the subject of the next entry.

27 Grooves II

SPACING

Between the Acts traces the course of a historical pageant at a country house on a summer's day. That may sound idyllic, but the idyll is willfully deceived about the cruelties underlying the history it reenacts, as Woolf's narrative makes painfully clear. Presiding over the festivities is a gramophone hidden behind some bushes. Its role in the pageant is to supply background music; its role in the novel is to provide a dark choral commentary through the "chuffing" and "ticking" of its needle in the grooves.

The full force of this noise, and its counterparts in Huxley and Flanagan, is best appreciated via the concept of "spacing" developed first by Jacques Derrida and subsequently by Jean-Luc Nancy. The names are formidable but the concept is simple. Any articulate expression needs space between its units: between written or printed words, for example, or, smaller but still present, between the letters that compose the words. Speech needs similar breaks between words and syllables. In most situations, such spacing passes largely unnoticed. But when something calls attention to it, spacing undercuts articulation; it becomes a kind of fracture that potentially opens into an abyss. Derrida says that it introduces death into the utterance; Nancy celebrates a resonance that can fill the space and keep the void at bay.[1]

Groove noise from a phonograph exposes spacing as a void. In *Between the Acts,* the sound in the groove becomes elegy; its chuffing noise, the sound of meaninglessness, alternates with a ticking noise, the sound of telling the time. The needle in the groove seems to be "saying," and to be saying over and over, "Dispersed are we." The word order says as much as the words: this is not ordinary language but poetry stood on its head. The undertone of lament, the shroud of the audible, extends everywhere: to the machine that chuffs and ticks; to the ellipses in the text; and to the valedictory in which groove noise triumphs and releases a flood of textual spaces between fragmentary utterances:

> *Dispersed are we,* the gramophone triumphed, yet lamented, *Dispersed are we. . . .*
>
> "But you must remember," the old cronies chatted, "they had to do it on the cheap. You can't get people, at this time o' year, to rehearse. There's the hay, let alone the movies. . . . What we need is a centre. Something to bring us all together . . . The Brookes have gone to Italy, in spite of everything. Rather rash? . . . If the worst should come—let's hope it won't—they'd hire an aeroplane, so they said. . . . What amused me was old Streatfield, feeling for his pouch. I like a man to be natural, not always on a perch . . . Then those voices from the bushes. . . . Oracles? You're referring to the Greeks? Were the oracles, if I'm not being irreverent, a foretaste of our own religion? Which is what? . . . Crepe soles? That's so sensible . . . They last much longer and protect the feet. . . . But I was saying: can the Christian faith adapt

itself? In times like these . . . At Larting no one goes to church . . . There's the dogs, there's the pictures. . . . It's odd that science, so they tell me, is making things (so to speak) more spiritual . . . The very latest notion, so I'm told is, nothing's solid . . . There, you can get a glimpse of the church through the trees. . . .[2]

The stippled page and broken utterance confirm the observation by Miss La Trobe, the artist who operates the phonograph, that it is death when illusion fails. Instead of dead silence, of spacing as void, the gramophone in Woolf exposes the positive sound of death, the sound of spacing itself, which without the needle in the groove would remain inaudible. The reader is asked to "hear" this sound as continuously present in the ellipses that space the voices into a jumble, each utterance making sense in itself but the totality making no sense at all.

The impression of hearing "*Dispersed are we*" in particular—really hearing it, despite the absence of real words—culminates as the pageant ends. The phrase arises in the wake of two closely preceding events. In one, an unidentifiable voice abruptly "asserts itself" on the gramophone to excoriate everyone within earshot ("*Liars most of us. Thieves too.*") Then, with equal abruptness, the voice reverses itself and offers recorded music as a source of affirmation—what music, exactly, remains unknown and does not matter. Whatever it is, it almost gets lost in the shuffle: "The records had been mixed. Fox trot, Sweet lavender, Home Sweet Home, Rule Britannia—sweating profusely, Jimmy, who had charge of the music, threw them aside and fitted the right one—was it Bach, Handel, Beethoven, Mozart or nobody famous, but merely a traditional tune?"[3] The musical respite is real but it is also fleeting. Once it is over, the local vicar makes an unctuous fundraising appeal to the audience only to have the word *opportunity* "cut in two" by the noise of a squadron of warplanes passing overhead.

Shortly afterward the gramophone likewise has an utterance cut in two. Resuming its leitmotif, "*Dispersed are we*," it adds the injunction, "*[but] let us retain whatever made that harmony*," presumably the harmony of the music offered by the unknown voice. But the plea for harmony disappears as soon as it is heard. In a sense it is never really heard. As the spectators of the pageant disperse indeed, only the recurrent knell of "*Dispersed are we*" remains to usher them away until a still more broken utterance silences the garrulous gramophone itself: "The gramophone gurgled *Unity—Dispersity*. It gurgled *Un* .. *dis* . . . And ceased."[4] As in the famous passage in Shakespeare's *The Tempest* that hovers behind this episode, the dissolution of the insubstantial pageant leaves not a rack behind. A little later Woolf draws our attention to the material heaviness of the recordings, the bulky 78 rpm disks in Miss La Trobe's backpack. The music in the air of the pageant has returned to its source: inert matter now wrapped in silence.

28 Beyond Analogy

In the fifteenth and sixteenth centuries Europe drew on classical sources to create a picture of the world, indeed of the cosmos, as a vast network of analogies. Resemblance, according to Michel Foucault, was the underlying principle not only of knowledge but also of being.[1]

Early in the present century Kaja Silverman revived this world picture in a new form. Analogy for Silverman does not depend on resemblance in the usual sense of the term. It is neither a logical nor a rhetorical relationship. It is, instead, the inherent connectivity, the "authorless and untranscendable" power, that allows me to refer one thing to another.

For Silverman, one particular mode of analogy, the visual, and more particularly the photographic, is preeminent: "Photography isn't a medium that was invented by three or four men in the 1820s and 1830s. . . . It is, rather, the world's primary way of revealing itself to us—of demonstrating that it exists, and that it will forever exceed us."[2] The world consists of photographs of itself. Without them it would remain undisclosed, hidden, not really a world at all. What we know, whatever we know, comes primarily from photographs in this extended sense of the term. Analogy gives "ontological weight" to the knowledge that results. Thus, for example, the fixed two-dimensional photograph of a face, even in color, does not really look much like the mobile three-dimensional face itself. The fixity and flatness of the image might even be said to caricature what it purports to show. Analogy is the principle (for Silverman, the miracle) that allows me to say that one *looks like* the other, or even *just like you,* and not be wrong.

But surely something similar could be said at least of sound and touch. Sound and touch, too, are ways that the world discloses itself to us, or better, brings us into concrete relationship with it, since we usually experience the world more as what is given than what is hidden. Why, then, is Silverman's model of knowledge, like most of our models of knowledge, at least in the West, still based on vision? Can we keep the miracle of analogy without constantly taking pictures?

An answer may suggest itself if we start by taking touch out of the equation. Touch is limited by proximity; it requires the annulment of distance. Only sight and hearing cross the distance. We have to stand back to see something clearly. We hear events behind our backs or too far away to see. Touch provides sensation, not knowledge, though it can become a *source* of knowledge when we reflect on or interpret it. But if sound, like sight, is at home in the distance, then why does sight have priority? Does it really?

To get an answer here we need to remind ourselves that sight and hearing are not opposites; they are rivalrous partners. They work together all the time but also contend at times for precedence. So why is this relationship between nominal equals still tilted in favor of sight? And what are we missing by letting it remain that way?

One reason may be the desire for immediacy. Since certainty is so often unattainable, we look for a vividness that can stand in for it: we want to know things *directly.* Sight in everyday life is a perfect model for such knowledge. Only in exceptional or unfamiliar circumstances do we feel the need to interpret what we see; we just see it; we recognize it; we know it. It's right in front of our eyes. The security of such seeing may offer some insight into the value of visual art, which productively upsets the visual field by turning it to something that must be interpreted if it is to be well seen.

Hearing, by contrast, requires interpretation all the time. Sounds that occur outside the visual field, so-called acousmatic sounds, fill our everyday experience. And those sounds all require a brief moment of interpretation, if only to locate their source. They often entail an immediate decision or value judgment. This sensory dimension of the heard world carries over, resonates, into speech, which with perfect fluidity vacillates between apparent self-evidence and the need to interpret.

What to make of this difference depends—odd though it seems to say so—on one's attitude toward metaphysics. If one believes that pure truth, meaning, or understanding is possible, however aspirational or rare, the visual model of knowledge is likely to remain primary. But if one believes that knowledge is not something to be found but something that is continuously in the process of being made and unmade, an ever-changing direction in the flow of reference or analogy, then the model changes. This is not a matter of sound seizing pride of place, but of visual analogy and auditory reference or resonance becoming genuinely equal and equally available. The world presents itself to us in both forms, more often simultaneously than not. And recognizing this opens the door to the kinds of attention to the world that this volume and *The Hum of the World* seek to exemplify.[3]

29 Phonogram and Gramophone

Thomas Edison rightly thought that recorded sound would have many uses, but he was not always right about which of them would flourish. One of these failed uses is especially revealing: the sending of a voice message recorded on an Edison cylinder in lieu of a telegram. The phonogram, as it was called, fizzled out quickly, done in partly by factors of cost and speed, and partly by a problem with packaging: it proved difficult to design a secure mailing container for the delicate cylinders. About the only legacy of the phonogram was a brief vogue early in the twentieth century for "talking postcards" on which prerecorded celluloid disks were glued.[1] In the first flush of enthusiasm, however, the Edison Company's London agent George Gouraud, a figure we have met before, set up a transatlantic testimonial. He invited his son-in-law, an American poet with the unlikely name of Horatio Nelson Powers, to compose a poem about the phonograph and to post his own voice recording of it from the Edison laboratories in Orange, New Jersey, to Gouraud's home in Surrey. The recording was made, and presumably sent, on June 16, 1888, accompanied by a folded sheet of paper (figure 2).

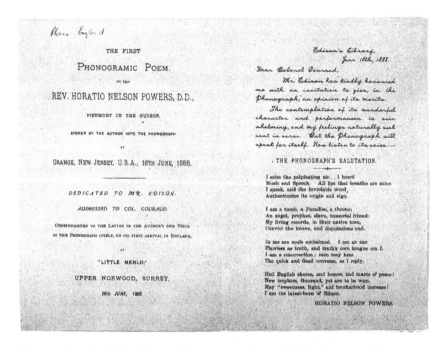

Figure 2. Horatio Nelson Powers, Phonogramic Poem (1888). Courtesy of the Thomas Edison Papers, Digital Edition.

The paper is the chief point of interest. It is divided in half along the fold. On the left side is a notice identifying the poem, author, date, and so on, in the manner of the title page of a book. On the right side, which is divided roughly into top and bottom halves, a handwritten message, very clearly legible, perches atop the text of the poem. The handwriting acts as a second introduction. But it introduces the printed text not as something to be read, but as something to be heard, and heard, moreover, when the phonogram recites the poem in its, the phonograph's, own voice: the phonograph will "speak for itself." The handwritten segment concludes with the invitation or injunction, "Now listen to its voice."

Powers's reference to the phonograph's voice strangely elides his own voice, which is, after all, the voice that recites the poem. As Jason Camlot has observed, Powers identifies the author—that is, himself in his capacity as an author—with the medium, the phonograph. The phonograph thus "gains its identity, its agency, its status as subject in a sentence . . . by its ability to stand in and communicate for the author in *its* own voice (ambiguity intended)."[2] If so, then the voice that has been recorded *loses* its identity, or at least that part of itself which marks its "ownness." The voice on the phonograph is not exactly the speaker's, but it cannot be the voice of anyone else.

What voice, then, does the listener hear? Whose is it? Does the machine preserve the person's voice, or transcribe it, or appropriate it, or replace it?

No one answer is possible, but the questions send us back to that sheet of paper. Each of the paper's three segments contains a different textual medium, as if to cover the full range of possibilities: display in multiple type-faces, text in a uniform typeface, text in handwriting. The paper groups the three together with the express purpose of declaring their obsolescence in view of the latest phase in the history of communications technology. The recording is supposed to remedy the deficits of printed text as printed text had formerly remedied the deficits of handwriting. The technologies continue to coexist, but their status and character change. The new technology underscores the inadequacies of text as a means of voice recording. In particular it is not enough to read Powers's poem, despite its clear presence on the page. The poem remains unwritten until it is heard, not just in its author's voice, but also in the voice of the phonograph. The recording is in this one respect more alive than the living voice—more alive and more durable.

Or is it? The multiplication of these textual formats may seem a little excessive. Perhaps more than a little. Their elaboration may testify to an unacknowledged anxiety; reading left to right and down the page, they lead us to the text of the poem, signed in type. In print, the poem is a safe-guard. It can also "speak for itself" in case the phonograph fails—if the phonographic voice is not fully or readily intelligible or not lifelike enough. Although it is hard to say how the cylinder would have sounded at the time, and to nineteenth-century ears, the sound quality of the surviving recording is very poor. The voice fades in and out and the recording is blurred by heavy groove noise. The grand claims made by the poem are undermined by the sounds that enunciate them.

Those claims form another point of interest. It is hard to know how seriously to take their grandiosity; the poem is in effect a high-toned advertisement and its hyperbole is surely meant to whip up sales. But Powers's elaborate verbal-visual design suggests that he took himself very seriously, and it therefore seems reasonable to draw out the implications of his language. This is especially true of the first three stanzas—for this text celebrating the new is quite traditional in its verse form—the language of which is straight-out apocalyptic.

Strangely for a poem in praise of a machine, "The Phonograph's Salutation" makes no reference to its speaker's mechanical condition except, indirectly, in the last line—and even there the image is one of birth, not of invention. The talking phonograph presents itself as alive, as if it did not *know* it is a machine. It even presents itself as immortal, its life as implicitly divine. Its "inviolable word" reenacts the Word that created the world; its voice makes the Logos audible. The sound of the phonograph transmits and authenticates the truth at the same time, joining the origin and sign of its speech into a single, endlessly reproducible speech act. It resurrects dead voices while at the same time—and here is where the hyperbole gets tangled in its own net, just as the phonographic ear is also a tongue—it "hoards" speech and becomes a tomb for "embalmed souls."

The inflated rhetoric is absurd, at least from a twenty-first-century standpoint, but its absurdity is just what needs explanation. We might suppose that the astonishment produced by early recorded sound on its listeners pushed their language about it to extremes. What that language reveals, though, at least in Powers's case, is the need to protect religion from the challenge of scientific rationality—one of the best-known challenges of the nineteenth century. While Powers signs his poem with his name, his "title page" prints his own title as well: "Rev. Horatio Nelson Powers, D.D." His answer to the unspoken challenge is to make the phonograph speak in the language of theology. The machine, unaware that it is not really alive, uses its nonetheless living voice, which also happens to be Powers's voice, to authenticate the "origin and sign" of true belief. The phonograph speaks as if it, too, were a doctor of divinity.

30 Forest Murmurs

One of the chief ways in which we experience the audiable is as the just-audible difference between quiet and silence, often heard in the motion of the air or the flow of water. In his poem "Airey-Force Valley" (1842), referring to a scenic retreat in England's Lake District, Wordsworth described how this attunement of the ear to the world occurs. Unlike his friend Coleridge, who liked going to concerts and is on record as admiring Mozart and Beethoven, Wordsworth does not seem to have taken much interest in music. But he was acutely sensitive to sound:

> —Not a breath of air
> Ruffles the bosom of this leafy glen.
> From the brook's margin, wide around, the trees
> Are steadfast as the rocks; the brook itself,
> Old as the hills that feed it from afar,
> Doth rather deepen than disturb the calm
> Where all things else are still and motionless.
> And yet, even now, a little breeze, perchance
> Escaped from boisterous winds that rage without,
> Has entered, by the sturdy oaks unfelt,
> But to its gentle touch how sensitive
> Is the light ash! that, pendent from the brow
> Of yon dim cave, in seeming silence makes
> A soft eye-music of slow-waving boughs,
> Powerful almost as vocal harmony
> To stay the wanderer's steps and soothe his thoughts.

The almost silent glen turns out to be filled, very quietly, with sound in continuous metamorphosis. The sound of the brook is the only one that can unambiguously be said to reach the ear. This sound, however, becomes audible not in itself but as a resonance within the prevailing stillness. The sequestered glen becomes a kind of ear in which the barely discernible sound of the audiable blends the present and the remote past into a single, long, hushed moment.

Then the moment segues into another. When the little breeze enters the glen, it bypasses hearing for touch, rustling the leaves on the ash boughs "in seeming silence." Sight at once tracks the motion, only to find that what it sees is music. The poem gives us no reason not to take this statement literally. The eye sees what the mind hears; the silence is only an appearance; sight becomes an auditory medium. The voiceless but quasi-vocal harmony of the boughs stays the wanderer's steps, something that is traditionally done by the "voice" of memorial inscriptions. Here, however, the *memento mori* becomes a *memento vitae*. The eye-music soothes the wanderer's thought precisely because it fills a space that would otherwise be filled with a silence portending death. Meanwhile, as the verse in the second half of the poem begins to spill over from one line to the next, the reader is encouraged to remember that the sound of the brook is still present in its transmuted form. If the breeze is strong enough to stir the ash boughs, it can go unheard only if it is covered by the murmur of the brook. For the time being, that murmur is the hum of the world.

31 Epithet

Like James Joyce in *Ulysses,* a book she claimed to find déclassé, Virginia Woolf in *Between the Acts* invests the single day of the narrative with wide-ranging significance. Unlike Joyce, she interrupts the progress of the day with moments of startling brutality: a veteran of the Indian army berating a little boy, his grandson, for unmanly cowardice; a philandering husband crushing a toad with his foot and bloodying his white shoes; and the day's impresario, Miss La Trobe, abruptly voicing the most infamous of racial epithets: "I was working like a —." (There is no need to print the word here.) Even during "silent" reading, the sheer *sound* of the word cuts through the text's aesthetic surface. It shouts down the "unconventional," "experimental" literariness of the writing. It disrupts even the text's criticism of class and empire. It defaces the page, not only because it gives offense but also because it is so incongruous; there is nothing else in the book remotely comparable. The use of the word is violent as well as vile.

Whether this is deliberate or not is hard to say. Miss La Trobe is the pariah from whom the narrative derives. She masterminds a pageant that has no room for her; she remains unseen; she enjoys no hospitality; she receives no thanks. Miss La Trobe is the object of bigotry because she is stocky, drinks too heavily, and has a "foreign" name, not to mention being a lesbian. But this is not to say that she, or her author, cannot also be complicit in bigotry. The word she uses is both a cry of resentment and a cry of defiance. Miss La

Trobe is not a colonial subaltern—in context the epithet refers to dark-skinned Indians, not Black Americans—and she thinks she should not be treated like one. But she does not object to the category; she only detests being placed in it. Like her chosen slur, Miss La Trobe has no proper place in the narrative, which her utterance brings to a momentary halt.

This episode may be more disturbing in 2021, as I write, than it was eighty years earlier, when the offensive term was in more common use. As the linguist John McWhorter has observed, racial and other stigmatizing epithets have recently assumed the prohibited status formerly occupied by terms referring to sexual organs and acts.[1] One can almost catch an early moment of transition in John Dos Passos's 1925 novel *Manhattan Transfer*. As in Woolf, the epithet comes out of the blue from a woman at odds with the gender norms of her community.[2] Here too the speaker is involved with theatrics (she is an actress and dancer) and has unconventional sexual habits (she is a "loose" woman). Like Miss La Trobe, Dos Passos's character, who changes names as readily as she does sexual partners, uses the racial slur to refuse being placed in the category it invokes while leaving the category intact.

But *Manhattan Transfer* is full of ethnic slurs; it makes Joyce look prim. The point is to represent just how pervasive ethnic categorization was in 1920s America. The sound of these words—and, again, it is a matter of sound—of words that become earworms even though not read aloud, is so resonant that the publisher of a new edition in 2021 felt obliged to include a cautionary note: "This book was published in 1925 and reflects the attitudes of its time. The publisher's decision to present it as it was originally published is not intended as endorsement of any offensive cultural representations and/or language."[3]

32 Mesmerizing Sound

In Book X of his *Republic,* Plato says that the order of the cosmos produces a perfect musical harmony—the music of the spheres, as it would come to be called. The spheres are those of the planets of classical astronomy, the five that can be seen by the naked eye, plus the sun, moon, and fixed stars. The celestial bodies orbit "the spindle of Necessity" (in later versions replaced by the earth) in concentric circles. Atop each sphere a heavenly siren sings a single note that harmonizes with the others to form a pure consonance, an "undisturbéd song of pure concent."[1]

The quotation comes from John Milton's "At a Solemn Musick" (1645), which draws on Christianized forms of the classical idea. Early Christian writers were quick to identify the *harmonia mundi,* the harmony of the world, with either the Word of creation or with the sound that greeted it "when the morning stars sang together, and all the sons of God shouted for joy" (Job 38:7, KJV). In 1687 John Dryden combined the two associations in the poem he wrote for the annual celebration of the patron saint of music held in London between 1683 and 1703, "A Song for St. Cecilia's Day":

> From harmony, from Heav'nly harmony
> > This universal frame began.
> > When Nature underneath a heap
> > Of jarring atoms lay,
> > And could not heave her head,
> The tuneful voice was heard from high,
> > Arise ye more than dead.
> Then cold, and hot, and moist, and dry,
> > In order to their stations leap,
> > > And music's pow'r obey.
> From harmony, from Heav'nly harmony
> > This universal frame began:
> > From harmony to harmony
> Through all the compass of the notes it ran,
> > The diapason closing full in man. (st. 1)

Although Henry Purcell composed a St. Cecilia's Day ode in 1692 to a text based on Dryden's, and George Frideric Handel in 1739 set Dryden's poem itself, neither composer tried to reproduce the sound of heavenly harmony. Handel would content himself with illustrating Dryden's language—jarring harmonies for jarring atoms—but Purcell sought to symbolize the sound he could not capture. His music for the lines "Thou tun'st this world below, the spheres above / Which in the heav'nly round to their own music move" occurs three times in succession: first for hautboys (early oboes) and bass, then for solo voice and bass, and then for chorus and bass. The tuning spreads from one sphere to another like an echo that grows stronger rather than weaker as it resounds. Within each of these concentric musical rings, the music for the second syllable of "above" turns, upon repetition, to a chord both bright and surprising, as if to cross from the earthly sphere to something higher. The chord gives sensory form to the symbolic realization of attunement.

Still, symbolism isn't sound, even if the symbol acts by sounding. Purcell's detour through musical metaphor implicitly acknowledges the traditional understanding that earthly music could at best be a distant echo of its heavenly model, which is inaudible to human ears. Or at least it *was;* in 1761 something changed.

That was the year in which Benjamin Franklin invented a new musical instrument, the glass armonica; the original is still extant, on display in Philadelphia at the Franklin Institute. The armonica consists of a series of tuned glass bowls mounted on a spindle—shades of Plato's spindle of necessity—rotated by a foot pedal. The performer plays the instrument like a keyboard, pressing on the bowls with moistened fingers.

The sound of the instrument struck many listeners as unprecedented— literally unlike any musical sound previously heard, including the sound of the tuned wine glasses on which Franklin had meant to improve. For some, the armonica's timbre grated on the nerves, to the point of inducing melancholy or even madness. One well-known friend of the Mozart family felt, on the contrary, that it soothed the nerves, and used it as part of the proto-hypnotic therapy known as mesmerism. This was Franz Anton Mesmer himself, who was an accomplished performer on the glass armon- ica. His composer friend Mozart also found the sound appealing. In the last year of his life Mozart composed two pieces for glass armonica after hearing a concert by the blind pianist Marianne Kirchgessner. Kirchgessner had become a virtuoso on the instrument, which even more than the key- board is played by touch.

Mesmer's idea that the sound of the armonica induced harmony in the body's "animal magnetism" pointed to harmony of a grander sort. Enthusiasts of the armonica frequently described its sound as unearthly, celestial, akin to the music of the spheres. In 1787 the composer Friedrich

Franz Hurka published a musical setting of a poem in praise of the instrument. The poem, its author identified only as "Richter," invokes both cosmic harmony and angelic song:

> When first each listening ear
> Hearkened to this novel tone
> Every child of earth
> Grew lost in rapture.
> The intoxicated spirit thought it could hear
> High harmonies of the spheres
> And the angels' song
> Praising the Uncreated.[2]

In 1810 E. T. A. Hoffmann wrote a hybrid text, half tale, half essay, called "Automata," which criticizes the then-current vogue for mechanical instruments. But Hoffmann makes an exception for the glass armonica:

> When humankind as yet was dwelling in its pristine holy harmony with nature . . . Mother Nature . . . encompassed him with a holy music, like the afflatus of a continual inspiration. . . . There has come down to us an echo from the mysterious depths of those primeval days—that beautiful notion of the music of the spheres. . . . I often used to listen, on quiet moonlight nights, to hear if those wondrous tones would come to me. [Their] swelling and gradual dying . . . has a most powerful and indescribable effect on us; and any instrument capable of producing this [sonority] would no doubt affect us similarly. . . . I think the armonica comes closest, in its tone, to that perfection.[3]

From this high point the instrument fell fairly quickly into obscurity, more or less disappearing by around 1820. Perhaps it declined because its sound is too easily covered. Or perhaps the reason was simple habituation. The sound was only celestial until one got used to it.

Its last star turn was one that didn't happen. In 1815 Beethoven wrote incidental music for a historical drama, *Leonora Prohaska*, celebrating a woman warrior who, disguised as a man, had died heroically in the struggle against Napoleon. The play went unproduced. Had it been staged, audiences would have encountered a short scene in which Leonora's spirit returns to earth to comfort her grieving beloved. Beethoven composed the scene for speaking voice and glass armonica. At first the armonica simply introduces Leonora's words, but its sound holds steady as she concludes. Beethoven writes out the instruction to sustain the sound behind her last words. In context, the voice seems to emanate from, momentarily to make articulate, the heavenly harmony into which it subsequently fades. The actual music to this scene is so simple as to be virtually negligible. The point is not the notes or the chords but their timbre alone.

A few decades later the British poet Felicia Hemans imagined a similar scene. In "A Spirit's Return" (ca. 1845) the lost beloved, a man this time, returns to console the woman who mourns him. He is described as speaking to her but we never know what he says:

How shall I tell thee of the startling thrill
In that low voice. . . . Soft, solemn, clear,
Breathed the mysterious accents on mine ear,
Yet strangely seemed as if the while they rose
From depths of distance, o'er the wide repose
Of slumbering waters wafted, or the dells
Of mountains, hollow with sweet echo-cells.[4]

Here again the point is not the message but the sound that conveys it. The depths of distance and hollow echo-cells are waystations of the audiable.

33 Cathay

In 1921 Amy Lowell and Florence Ayscough published a volume entitled *Fir-Flower Tablets: Poems Translated from the Chinese*. Ayscough was born in Shanghai to Canadian and American parents and lived most of her life there. She is listed as the translator of the poems in the volume, but the texts are "English versions" credited to Lowell, who wrote in the preface that her "long and arduous" task was "to turn [Ayscough's] literal translations into poems as near to the spirit of the originals as it was in my power to do."[1] The majority of the poems are by the Tang Dynasty poet then generally known as Li Po, here identified as Li T'ai-Po, and now generally known as Li Bai (701–762 CE).

The print edition, as the editor of the digitized version explains, contained numerous explanatory notes, but there were no indications in the text linking passages in the poems to the notes that explain them. The notes' invisibility allows the translations to assume a "Chinese" esotericism wholly lacking in the originals. The names of places and persons become evocative sounds that invoke only distance without reference; sequences of simple statements with little or no transition suggest a depth of perception that summons—tantalizes—a reader who can never reach it. "Bidding Good-Bye to Yin Shu" is typical:

> Before the White Heron Island—the moon.
> At dawn to-morrow I shall bid good-bye to the returning traveller.
> The sky is growing bright,
> The sun is behind the Green Dragon Hill;
> Head high it pushes out of the sea clouds and appears.
> Flowing water runs without emotions,
> The sail which will carry him away meets the wind and fills.
> We watch it together. We cannot bear to be separated.
> Again we pledge each other from the cups we hold in our hands.

The exclusion of more complex grammatical constructions reinforces the impression of a mystical proximity to the world that contrasts favorably with the supposedly more abstract but therefore more alienated character of Western language and thought. What looks like an admiring embrace of Chinese culture, and actually is one, is nonetheless an appropriation meant to hold an unflattering mirror up to Western nature.

Lowell's model is Ezra Pound's book *Cathay* (1915), based on notes by the art historian Ernest Fenollosa and similarly concentrating on poems by Li Bai. The book supplies a famous example of imaginary esotericism in the poem "Separation on the River Kiang"—a beautiful lyric (one I have set to music) built in part on errors of translation, some of them deliberate. The first line, "Ko-jin goes west from Ko-kaku-ro," seems to begin with a proper name, but the Chinese phrase that the "name" transliterates actually means "old acquaintance." Yunte Huang has observed that Pound often conjures up proper names with such homophonic translations; doing so, however, cancels the power of reference in favor of incantation.[2] The proper names name only themselves. "Ko-jin" carries a mystique; "old acquaintance" would inhibit one. (Lowell proves the point by translating the phrase as "my dear old friend.")

The mystique continues in the alliterative "Ko-kaku-ro," literally Yellow Crane Tower, a famous landmark in Wuhan. The tower has repeatedly been destroyed and rebuilt over a span of millennia. That fact would add a layer of resonance to the translation, as it does to the original poem, but the translation means to exclude it. The transliterated sound rolls wonderfully on the tongue and also in a singing voice, and its aim is to do exactly that. Its effect is to mute the historical resonance of the landmark and to set the poem in the land of fable, long ago and far away and for that very reason always here and now.

34   Night. A Street. No Lamps.

Early in his historical novel *Barnaby Rudge,* Charles Dickens describes the streets of London at night as they looked in 1775. But "looked" is the wrong word because one could scarcely see anything. Dickens depicts the city as minimally illuminated and therefore maximally dangerous. Writing in 1841, he might as well have been looking back centuries as decades. Gaslight was introduced to London in 1807; by 1823 there were forty thousand lights in the city. Darkness had become peripheral; the urban night was no longer something to be shunned, at least in the less impoverished neighborhoods.

For Dickens, traveling the streets of the former age meant reorienting oneself from the absence of light to the presence of sound:

> Some of the shops . . . still adhered to the old practice of hanging out a sign; and the creaking and swinging of these boards in their iron frames on windy nights, formed a strange and mournful concert for the ears of those who lay awake in bed or hurried through the streets. Long stands of hackney-chairs and groups of chairmen, compared with whom the coachmen of our day are gentle and polite, obstructed the way and filled the air with clamour; night-cellars, indicated by a little stream of light crossing the pavement, and stretching out half-way into the road, and by the stifled roar of voices from below, yawned for the reception and entertainment of the most abandoned

of both sexes; under every shed and bulk small groups of link-boys gamed away the earnings of the day; or one more weary than the rest, gave way to sleep, and let the fragment of his torch fall hissing on the puddled ground.[1]

Unreadable for the time being, their names or images obscured, the shop signs transfer their signifying power to the sound of their boards, their solid matter, creaking in the wind. Or rather they translate their signification into a kind of music that links those who lie in bed with those who hurry through the streets—ultimately the quick and the dead. These are figures moved alike by a sound that is mysterious—its music no longer "means" anything—and all too familiar: the concert of voided signs is mournful, and mournfulness needs no translation. On the streets, the sound of voices signals the presence of a modern mouth of hell for those inclined to make the descent. Concealed in the darkness, a solitary linkboy, worn out by his work, gives way to a sleep that portends death, not in a sign, but in the sound of the guttering out of his torch in a puddle.

Common to all these sounds is a peculiar truthfulness. The creaking signboards remind the listener of the proverb that the wind bloweth where it listeth. When the linkboy's light goes out, the sound of its extinction measures the depth of his weariness. It is as if sound, left to its own devices, could not help revealing what might otherwise remain concealed.

35 The Resonating Cure

In Vienna, in 1825, the painter and sometime mesmerist Ludwig Schnorr von Carolsfeld called on a musical friend to help him tranquilize a problem patient. The patient was a woman who compulsively made indecorous sounds and who had increasingly come to resist yielding to the "magnetic sleep" required for her taming—in other words, her therapy. Her name was Louise Mora. The musical friend was Franz Schubert.[1]

Lacking Mesmer's glass armonica, Schnorr had tried to soothe Mora by playing "a few chords" on the piano. The chords came from a recently published German dance by Schubert (D. 783, No. 7). The chords seemed to go over well enough, so Schnorr asked Schubert to come to a subsequent session and play more. Schubert complied. We know he both played and sang, but we don't know for how long or what music was involved, except for that German dance. Mora was especially receptive to it, and when Schubert had played it through a second time—not hard to do, since it lasts only about a minute—she promptly obeyed his softly spoken injunction to sleep.

What was it about this unpretentious little piece that wrought such a large effect? The answer lies in Schubert's written instruction to play the whole thing "with lifted dampers"—in other words, with the sustaining pedal continuously pressed down (or, in the case of the knee pedal probably found on the early piano involved, pressed in). The sonority that results is a light auditory haze. This lingering, hovering resonance envelops the music but is not exactly a part of it. Its closest musical kin is the sound of the glass armonica, which continues to resonate faintly after the player's fingers leave the bowls and that accumulates as the playing continues. Just why Schubert asked for this sound remains a mystery. But Mora seems to have heard in it what Mesmer heard in the sound of the armonica, an objectified form of magnetic sleep. She could let go of her resistance because the music that emitted this sound was convivial. It made no demands and sought no depths. It was just pretty, which is exactly what it needed to be under the circumstances.

Schnorr's best-known painting, a depiction of St. Cecilia, the patron saint of music, has something of the same therapeutic mildness.[2] The painting depicts Cecilia placidly hovering in air. Her halo forms the center of four concentric circles whose light bands of color, rimmed in gold, give a visual impression of sonorous pulsation. A row of organ pipes below rhyme with the curve of the halo, marking the affinity between the instrumental sound—Cecilia was especially associated with the organ—and inner peace.

36 The Voice of Language

Martin Heidegger says that language, *as* language, makes the distant near. No matter what is said, its saying serves this end.[1] But the distance is not negated; it is changed. The nearness created by language is always the nearness of the distant, even when one speaks of things close by.

In writing of language *as* language, in asking what language "says," Heidegger has live speech in mind. It is as if the sound of the word within earshot acts as the medium in which the distant comes near. That makes sense; sound always spatializes; sound is the extension of an event into space. We hear the evidence of what we cannot see. Each particular sound we hear beckons us in its direction, even though sound is everywhere. The work of language is thus a matter of sensation when speech brings the distant near. The ear lightly tingles with it, or resonates if the speech is compelling. Correspondingly, when the distance belongs to time, the bringing near is a matter of memory, whether personal or historical. The sound of the word acts like a momentary restoration, or half of one, a trace of a bygone presence.

Well and good. But what happens if, instead of speech, we have writing in mind?

For one thing the element of memory intensifies. Speech is of the present moment; writing persists to be read at future moments. (So does recorded speech, which in that respect is essentially a form of writing, as the name of its first medium, the phonograph—attests.) Even in the future tense writing is historical in its bringing of nearness; nearness in writing is always a matter of memory. The process is inexorable. Written over a century ago, "I will arise and go now"—whether by Yeats or not—becomes the memory of a former future. Written today, any day, every *now* is already a *then*. We just agree not to notice most of the time, so that we can inhabit time and not just watch it pass.

With writing, however, the spatial-sensory aspect of nearness changes. It shifts to a form of sound more intimate but less tangible than external speech. The sensory nearness of writing *as* writing is the sound half heard in the mind's ear. This sound resembles the sound of one's inner voice in thinking, with the important difference that the voice one hears in reading originates with someone else. It is the voice of the writer as the voice of the writing. The proximity of *that* voice to the reader's own interior voice is what allows readers to feel personally touched by writing that feels special to them.

Until modern literary theory made it seem naive, readers commonly felt that reading was a means of hearing an author's voice, whether the author was living or dead and whether or not the text featured a fictional speaker or narrator. In Robert Browning's famous poem "My Last Duchess," the brutal duke does the speaking, but generations of readers heard Browning—the real, flesh-and-blood Browning—ventriloquizing the duke's voice. Understanding written voice as fictional has its advantages. It allows insight into the means and ends of the literary fiction and it encourages intellectual detachment. But the understanding is itself a form of fiction and it does not need to be adopted all the time. The voice in writing is not an illusion; it is a quasi-sensory phenomenon. Of course the author's voice is not "really" there in the usual sense of the term—but *something* is. And we depend on that something to ground the feeling of connection to the past recorded in every act of writing. The text is the groove of a different phonograph.

To which we might add that there is a further sensory aspect to writing that has no exact counterpart in speech, whether live or recorded. Speech is heard as it is uttered, but the writing of an inscription is separate from the reading of it. The *act* of writing, like the act of speaking, makes sounds; writing is not noisy, but it is audible. Just what sounds the act of writing makes depends on the implement of writing. The dependency is unavoidable, since writing always needs an implement; writing is never "natural." Granted, one might say the same of speech, which must be trained, which responds to the social-acoustic dimension of the spaces it inhabits, and which is always uttered in a context. But live speech, at least, does come directly from the body, as writing does not.

Does, then, the sound made by writing affect how the written text sounds to the writer's mind? To the reader's? The character of the sound varies with the implement: quill or nib and inkwell, fountain pen, pencil, ballpoint, typewriter, computer keyboard. But there is literally very little written on these questions. It is as if writing preferred to erase the sound of its making, the better to show the visual form of its lasting. The act of inscription is a mute command to read.

37   Nocturne. Another City.

In his semifictional memoir *Goodbye to Berlin,* Christopher Isherwood describes the soundscape of a tenement in the city's poorest district:

Lying in bed, in the darkness, in my tiny corner of the enormous human warren of the tenements, I could hear, with uncanny precision, every sound which came up from the courtyard below. The shape of the court must have acted as a gramophone horn. . . . Somewhere on the other side of the court a baby began to scream, a window was slammed to, something very heavy, deep in the innermost recesses of the building, thudded dully against a wall. It was alien and mysterious and uncanny, like sleeping out in the jungle alone.[1]

The courtyard as gramophone horn makes darkness audible, and not just the darkness of night. The sounds are all disturbing, some of them threatening. Aside from the screams of the baby, the slam of the window, and the dull, heavy thud—of what?—there are the violent coughing of Isherwood's hostess, the ominous muttering of her son in his sleep, the fading report of retreating footsteps (the space here leans toward absence on all sides), and the grating of a key in a lock followed by another slam, of a door this time. Misery and precarity reverberate; their sound in the darkness makes them even worse. Despite Isherwood's jungle image, this nightscape is strictly modern and urban, just as its ancestor is in Wordsworth's *The Prelude,* encountered in the Paris of 1792 in the wake of revolutionary violence:

> But at the best it seemed a place of fear,
> Unfit for the repose of night,
> Defenseless as a wood where tigers roam.[2]

A more nearly contemporaneous parallel occurs in Rainer Maria Rilke's poem "The Vast Night" (Die grosse Nacht, 1914). Rilke's imagery is remarkably close to Isherwood's, as if being "refused" by the city at night had an auditory logic of its own:

> Still this new city
> was as if refused to me, and the unpersuaded landscape
> grew dark there as if I didn't exist. The things nearby
> did not take the trouble to become intelligible for me.
> The alley thrust itself to the lamppost: I saw that it was alien.
> Over there—a room, palpable, clarified in lamplight—
> Already I took part; they sensed it and shut the shutters.
> Stood. And then a child cried. . . .

Or there sang a woman's voice and went a little way out
past expectation, or downstairs there coughed an old man
full of reproach, as if his body were in the right
against the milder world.[3]

Rilke's night is something like Isherwood's acoustic courtyard, a
medium that captures passing sounds and magnifies them. The image of
the gramophone intimates what happens in both texts: the city's noctur-
nal sounds play back as if recorded, but also as if the recording were an
act, not of preservation, but of erasure. The sounds mark only their own
departure, epitomized in Isherwood by the fading footsteps. Yet the con-
veyance of this transience through a gramophone horn also conveys the
certainty that similar sounds, the "same" sounds, can and will be heard in
the modern city on any night at all. Crying, a cough, a thud: they will
always be there, unmistakable but never quite decipherable. The gramo-
phone works in reverse. The sounds it transmits always hold something
back; they do not take the trouble to become intelligible. And that refusal
is the vastness of their night.

38 Annals of Slavery

A VIOLIN

Solomon Northup was a free Black man who was abducted by slave catch-
ers in Washington, DC, in 1841. He recorded what happened next in his
memoir (as told to David Wilson), *Twelve Years a Slave*, published in
1853 and widely read at the time. Northup endured slavery for the twelve
years of his title before finally regaining his freedom. He was also a violin-
ist, and he somehow managed to keep hold of his instrument during his
captivity. The violin lightened his servitude—sometimes—and he keeps
the reader mindful of its value to him. Oddly, though, he says little or
nothing about the *sound* of the violin. The one passage to the contrary
treats the instrument as the source and personification of a surrogate
human voice:

[The violin] was my companion. . . . Often, at midnight, when . . . my soul was disturbed and troubled with the contemplation of my fate, it would sing me a song of peace. On holy Sabbath days, when an hour or two of leisure was allowed, it would accompany me to some quiet place on the bayou bank, and, lifting up its voice, discourse kindly and pleasantly indeed.[1]

It is impossible to know how much of this language came from Northup and how much from Wilson, but in any case the published text (which Wilson says that Northup reviewed) represents the solitary playing of the violin as a kind of ventriloquism. The violin sings, but it also speaks; it has a companionable voice that discourses with the listener whose playing produces it. Soliloquy becomes dialogue. The violin sings to console the slave Northup has become; it speaks "kindly and pleasantly" to the free man he knows himself to be. The metaphor is more essential than the sounds that realize it. At the same time, by inserting these interludes of solitary performance into the narrative, Northup and Wilson reappropriate the violin from its abuse by the cruel enslaver Epps, who is described two chapters earlier. Epps makes the instrument a device of false, coercive jollity, forcing his slaves to dance to its tunes, exhausting them for his amusement. Epps commands enjoyment from the enslaved so that he can enjoy their enslavement.[2]

But perhaps the most revealing episode with the violin comes in the story of Celeste, a woman who appears to Northup out of nowhere, as if his music had conjured her up: "I was sitting in my cabin late at night, playing a low air on my violin, when the door opened carefully, and Celeste stood before me. She was pale and haggard. Had an apparition arisen from the earth, I could not have been more startled." Celeste quickly belies both her name and her wraithlike appearance. When the startled Northup asks, "Who are you?" she replies with a demand rather than an answer: "Give me some bacon. I'm hungry."[3]

Celeste, whose paleness stems partly from hunger and partly (though Northup does not say so) from an enslaving father, is a runaway. Northup continues to share food with her for most of a summer while she hides in a hut built of dead branches and palmetto leaves deep in the swamp. But Celeste has no violin to discourse with her. The swamp at night is filled with "the howlings of wild animals," and the sound eventually becomes too terrifying to endure. Celeste returns to her enslaver, who scourges her and sends her back to work in the fields.

After another incident of scourging in which he is forced to participate, the Northup of Steve McQueen's 2013 film *12 Years a Slave* violently destroys his violin, smashing it to pieces against a tree. The scourging incident really happened, but as far as we know the historical Northup kept his "beloved violin" safe from harm. Northup the person clung to the consoling power of music amid the worst enormities of slavery; Northup the character does violence to music because the enormities turn the consolations into lies.

39 The Grammar of Uncertainty

The audiable is an unbound term, that is, one that requires continual redefinition to retain its meaningfulness. The best-known examples of unbound terms tend to come from philosophers: *will to power* from Nietzsche, *care* from Heidegger, *face* from Levinas, *form of life* from Wittgenstein, *différance* from Derrida. Philosophical thought needs these terms, which form the link between a conceptual order and the world of experience. The pliancy of the terms allows each sphere to affect the other.

Unbound terms have meaning only in connection with the words around them. The experience they refer to becomes apprehensible as such only through their use. These terms act semantically the way words such as "all," "every," "some," and "much"—known in formal logic as "syncategorematic expressions"—act grammatically. Unbound terms become meaningful by altering the meaning of the bound terms in the discourse around them. Their effect resembles the effect of tone of voice on a word or phrase or sentence. Unlike their grammatical and tonal counterparts, however, unbound terms have denotations of their own. But the denotation of an unbound term is fluid. It remains indefinite until a given term is used, most often in multiple contexts. Thereafter it becomes indefinite again. It exists as a floating conception that is simultaneously intelligible and elusive. Or rather it is neither one nor the other but a continual wavering between the two.

In this respect, however, unbound terms are not unique. Instead they embody in concentrated form the fundamental disposition of language itself, which never stands still and would fail to communicate if it did. Although it is often practical to pretend otherwise, every statement is incomplete.

Just so, every impression of completion is momentary. The factor that seals those impressions, when they arise, is often sound: the placement of emphasis, the degree of force, the real or imagined tone of voice in which the statement finds utterance. In his *Philosophical Investigations,* Wittgenstein asks whether the sentence "I am leaving the room, but not because you tell me to" describes or creates the connection between the action of leaving and the order to leave.[1] The question is rhetorical; the connection would be indefinite if I left the room in silence. Nothing would be settled except the action. In that case *how* I left the room, including the sound of my footsteps, might take the place of speech. But since the sentence is in play, the connection is swept up in it. The connection depends on what the sentence means, and depending on how it is uttered, the sentence can mean what it says or exactly the opposite.

To make sure the reader understands him, Wittgenstein writes an emphatic tone into his own sentence. His question actually reads: "This sentence—does it *describe* a connection between my action and his order; or does it make the connection?"[2] So that is that, we might say. But once we understand all this we are left with everything that might remain to be said: What room? Whose room? Who is speaking? To whom? Who has the authority here? What authority? (The reader is invited to leave the room and write a play or novel by way of answer, which will in turn raise another host of questions.)

40 Aftersounds

There are many ways to make the audiable present musically. The pedal effect in Schubert's unexpectedly therapeutic German dances, heir to the timbre of the glass armonica, takes advantage of a new technological resource under cover of a minor work. But as Beethoven had shown in his Piano Sonata no, 17 in D Minor, op. 31, no. 2 (1801–2), the mechanism of the piano and the freedom of the player's hands open up a host of opportunities. At pivotal moments the sonata's first movement produces mysterious sounds that linger or float amid a faint resonating medium produced by the pedal, halting the impetuous rush of the music.[1] The great proliferation of music for solo piano in the century to follow stems in part from similar juxtapositions of human and mechanical invention.

In 2020–21 I composed a collection of piano etudes, half of which are named "Phantom Etudes" because their music inheres as much or more in what their sounds leave behind—their "aftersounds"—as it does in the sounds themselves. Sounds fading, lingering, or accumulating, sounds veiling or unveiling other sounds, sounds impinging on or dropping away from other sounds, all form a running counterpoint to the presence of "positive" notes and phrases. The "negative" sonorities produce a kind of shadow music that lingers alongside the positive sounds, envelops them, and changes their character.

Arvo Pärt's *Spiegel im Spiegel* (Mirror in the Mirror, 1978; the title can also be translated in the plural) also depends on a kind of shadow music. The piece forms a musical parallel to the multiplication of images produced when an image in one mirror is reflected in another. Here too the piano sustains an enveloping resonance, in this case more by the uniformity of its part than by pedaling, but its role is to stay in the background and fill acoustic space. The fulfillment of the title is left to the solo instrument that, except in one version for piano alone, the resonance supports. The mirror projection arises from the comings and goings of a single sound on the solo instrument, originally a violin: one note, always on the same pitch. The note is the A above middle C, and the choice of that particular note is significant. But before considering its import we need to account for the way the note comes and goes.

Spiegel im Spiegel is an early instance of what Pärt calls "tintinnabular" style, from *tintinnabulum*, Latin for bell. The style aims at absolute transparency; it consists of a tintinnabular voice arpeggiating a tonal triad ("the three notes of a triad," says Pärt, "are like bells") and another voice moving in diatonic steps up and down the associated scale. "The complex and many-faceted," Pärt has said, often merely confuses him; he needs a clarifying unity and finds it in the oneness of the voices dwelling respectively on the triad and its scale. The result is that "everything that is unimportant falls away."[2]

The violin in *Spiegel im Spiegel* spins out an ever-expanding melodic pattern. The music's central A belongs to the music's key (F major) but does not ground it. It forms an island of repose but not of perfect stability. Nor is it the first note we hear: the first note is G. The violin approaches the A first from the G below, then from the B-flat above: one note up, one down. The up-and-down pattern then continues (sometimes reversing into down-and-up) by aggregation: two notes up and down to A, then three, and so on throughout the piece.

The A is (thus) always present even when it is acoustically silent; the memory and foreknowledge of the sound is, becomes, the sound itself, its futurity a sensory presence, its periodic presence extending into the future. The music marks this extended presence by its managing of duration. The notes leading to and from the destination A move evenly; the note value (a dotted half note, as it happens) never changes. The A both anchors and jostles this steady motion; it is always two and half times longer than the notes entrained with it. At the destination points one hears with one's bodily ears the extension of the note that becomes mirrored to infinity in the mind's ear across the span of the work as a whole and, in principle, beyond it. The expansive repetition of the pattern extends the sound without thinning it; in principle again, as the title suggests, the extension could go on to infinity, always returning to the A that it in some sense never leaves.

The A involved, moreover, is not just any A. It is A_4—presumably A440, the A to which a modern orchestra tunes. The note is the audible measure of standard Western tuning and, by extension, of musical and mental attunement. The expansion to infinity is a material process but one that intimates a multiplication of mental states.

The difference of this music from my "Phantom Etudes" is worth noting, especially with the glass armonica and the music of the spheres in the historical background. Pärt's design, as with all his music, is spiritual; there is something hymnlike as well as hypnotic about *Spiegel im Spiegel*. One result has been a multiplicity of transpositions for solo instruments other than the violin, including even solo piano. The music aims at the elemental and universal; its element is divine mystery. My "Phantom Etudes," by contrast, are wholly secular. They are fluid whereas *Spiegel im Spiegel* is steady-state. The phantoms in these etudes are, so to speak, un-unearthly. They take the presence of material aftersounds as spirit enough and invite a meditative state by demanding attention not only to but also through and beyond the notes. The only thing mysterious about them is the enduring mystery of sensation itself: simple sentience. These differences, of course, say nothing about aesthetic value. Their significance lies primarily in the demonstration that the audiable takes no sides except the side of time to come. It simply is because it will simply be.

41 Persistence of Hearing

Sound, we're accustomed to saying, disappears in the moment of its arrival. This truism seems to derive from two sources: a tacit substitution of speech for sound and a tacit identification of sound with the passage of time. In a very modest sense, the idea of sound as a vanishing arrival is valid for these two instances. What sounds in this second must disappear for something to sound in the next. The articulation necessary for speech requires the same elapsing. Sound has to make room for itself. In common experience, however, neither form of transience assumes much importance, nor does either come to much notice, if any. When they do, it is an event. Nor can this background transience serve to distinguish sound from sight, since despite its relative stability the visual field is full of events that vanish in the act of happening: a bird flits by.

Speaking of birds: in the countryside, where I live, flocks of wild geese sometimes make a racket as they pass. You hear them before you see them, their honking makes a crescendo as they approach and a diminuendo after they pass, and the hubbub fades into the distance well after the geese are out of sight. The sound presents itself as a kind of solid; it persists like the pedal point of an organ or a drone bass. The sight presents itself as evanescent, the flock gone by almost as soon as it becomes visible. The time of sight passes more swiftly than the time of hearing.

The persistence of sound is thus inherent in its nature, in nature at large. But there is also second nature to be considered. Sound ceased to be a vanishing arrival on the day in 1877 when Thomas Edison finished inventing the phonograph. By that I do not mean simply to restate a plain fact in fancy form. The point is that once sound could be stored and retrieved for repetition in real time, the phenomenon of sound changed fundamentally. Its transience in the moment fused with the possibility of its later retrieval. The whole field of sound began to resonate with the questions of what had been recorded (or not), what should be (or not), and—since recording also immediately introduced the possibility, realized later on, of editing—what should be done with it (or not). At the same time, the apparent veracity of sound became unstable: could one believe one's ears any more than one's eyes? The parallel with the invention of photography is nearly exact.

Was this change also retrospective? Did it include the lost sounds of the apparently prerecorded past?

Not at the time, nor for a long time thereafter. The terms for raising the question perhaps had to wait for the system of machine-human interfaces that now grows with each passing day. But if we think of sound as inherently recordable, it becomes possible to look back—or should I say listen back?—to nonmechanical forms of sound recording and hear more in them than we once did. Consider John Stuart Mill's famous statement that lyric poetry is not heard but overheard. For Mill in 1833, reading a lyric was a form of listening. Whether a poem is read aloud or not, it puts the reader or listener in contact with the poet's authentic voice. It does so despite the intervention of lyric artifice in rhyme and meter and stanza, or rather, those elements of form become a kind of phonographic medium. The lyric artifice paradoxically reveals the writer's voice at its most artless. It records a voice "confessing itself to itself in moments of solitude, and embodying itself in symbols which are the nearest possible representations of the feeling in the exact shape in which it exists in the poet's mind."[1]

Sometimes one could even hear more than one voice. Here is John Keats, in a famous sonnet of 1816 celebrating his discovery of Homer's voice through the Elizabethan translation by George Chapman:

Oft of one wide expanse had I been told
　　That deep-browed Homer ruled as his demesne;
　　Yet never did I breathe its pure serene
Till I heard Chapman speak out loud and bold:

Then felt I like some watcher of the skies
    When a new planet swims into his ken;
Or like stout Cortez when with eagle eyes
    He stared at the Pacific—and all his men
Looked at each other with a wild surmise—
    Silent, upon a peak in Darien.[2]

Keats's intertwined metaphors record that he became able to *see* the formerly undiscovered world of Homer when he could *hear* Chapman transmitting Homer's voice. The relay of voices is auditory—"loud and bold"—even if the ear that hears it is only the mind's. Keats, speaking in his own voice (the idea of a fictitious speaker or literary persona could not be further away) reenacts the moment of discovery, both his and the Pacific explorers', by ending the poem with the onset of silence. This silence is double. On the one hand it is the silence of the reader's voice when the mind's ear is filled with the voice of the author; on the other hand it is the silence of the poet's voice that will follow in a moment when the reading has ended. In this case the reader of one poet (or two, since this is Chapman's Homer) has become the poet for another reader. The relay of voices continues as Keats speaks out loud and bold.

The impression of written voice was robust. In the nineteenth century, the great age of expanding literacy, it extended to literary prose as well. From there it passed to the desire of readers to hear living authors— Dickens, Baudelaire, Whitman, Wilde—verify their written with their spoken voices. But with the advent of mechanically recorded voice, the impression of written voice attenuates, and not just because literary critics discredit it. With recorded voice ubiquitous, the acoustic becomes the sole measure of vocality. The popularity of audiobooks would seem proof enough of that. And when the reader of an audiobook is not the author, we want the reading voice to sound the way the author's should. But then, when the reader of an audiobook *is* the author, we still want the reading voice to sound the way the author's should.

Was the written voice "really there" in an earlier era? That is the wrong question. If we ask whether the voice could be heard when recorded in writing, the answer is: "Yes. But not acoustically." At one time, written voice was what phenomenology calls an intentional object, something that presents itself to consciousness in a certain way. And then it wasn't.

42 Annals of Slavery II

A VIGIL

The 2018 horror movie *A Quiet Place* is set in a postapocalyptic world in which human beings must keep silent to avoid being killed by alien creatures with acutely sensitive ears. I doubt that the filmmakers thought of this plot as an allegory of slavery in the antebellum South, but it is a perfectly good allegory for at least one celebrated case. In her memoir *Incidents in the Life of a Slave Girl* (1861), Harriet Jacobs describes her confinement for nearly seven years in the attic crawl space of her grandmother's house. She took refuge in this necessarily quiet place from her enslaver's attempts to coerce her into serving him sexually. The coercion was intolerable even though it was psychological, not physical; Jacobs's "Dr. Flint"—the name a well-chosen pseudonym—preferred a softer form of rape. He wanted to break Jacobs's will to resist, and he persisted the more she refused him. In the end, disappearance was the only solution, and it took Jacobs seven years of hiding before she could disappear into the North.

Forced into silence, she became acutely sensitive to sound. Unlike the characters in the film, however, Jacobs experienced sound not as a threat to life but as the thread that linked her to it:

> Morning came. I knew it only by the noises I heard; for in my small den day and night were all the same. I suffered for air even more than for light. But I was not comfortless. I heard the voices of my children. There was joy and there was sadness in the sound. It made my tears flow. How I longed to speak to them! I was eager to look on their faces; but there was no hole, no crack, through which I could peep. This continued darkness was oppressive. It seemed horrible to sit or lie in a cramped position day after day, without one gleam of light. Yet I would have chosen this, rather than my lot as a slave, though white people considered it an easy one; and it was so compared with the fate of others.[1]

At night Jacobs was occasionally able to snatch a few moments of conversation with members of her family. Eventually she came across a gimlet and was able to bore a small hole in the wall through which she could see the street. The respite was welcome, but real consolation still took the form of sound and reached its limit in the lack of sound:

> In the morning I watched for my children. The first person I saw in the street was Dr. Flint. I had a shuddering, superstitious feeling that it was a bad omen. Several familiar faces passed by. At last I heard the merry laugh of children, and presently two sweet little faces were looking up at me, as though they knew I was there, and were conscious of the joy they imparted. How I longed to *tell* them I was there![2]

This description is perhaps best taken as a symbolic reconstruction, given the passage from the sight of Dr. Flint to the sound of Jacobs's children, and the language of the children's "merry laugh" and "sweet little faces," which is reminiscent of the domestic fiction highly popular at the time. Jacobs is more plainspoken elsewhere, as in her earlier comment that the sound of her children's voices brought her both joy and sadness, and her subsequent observation that, although her voice could never be allowed to reach the children, their voices could sometimes reach her: "The heat of my den was intense. . . . But I had my consolations. Through my peeping-hole I could watch the children, and when they were near enough, I could hear their talk."[3] Jacobs can also overhear conversations that would normally not reach her ears: the plans of slave hunters, debates over whether she herself should be hunted ("'I wouldn't move my little finger to catch her, as old Flint's property'"), and the general opinion that she had escaped to freedom.[4] Until that escape became possible, what freedom she had was carried on the sound of voices in the street.

43   A Voice in a Box

In his *Sinister Resonance: The Mediumship of the Listener,* David Toop proposes that sound is inherently spectral, "out of sight, out of reach." Sound is "void, fear, and wonder."[1] But is it? Well, sometimes, yes, of course. Toop gives a wealth of examples. But inherently? Surely not. Sound is ordinary; more than that, sound is the foundation of the ordinary, even more than sight is. Void and fear, if not wonder, rush in where sound is nullified. The sense of the world is carried on vibration. (Deafness does not change this, though it makes it more complicated.) As the quoted phrases suggest, Toop finds sound uncanny because he is measuring it by visual standards. We cannot see through walls, but there is nothing surprising in our ability to hear through walls. We can't see in a dreamless sleep, but sleeping ears can hear, and there is nothing strange about it. The ordinary is not the same as routine. Nor as dullness. Nor as boredom. It may become uncanny, and often does; a disposition to become strange is part of being ordinary; a measure of strangeness is usual. But the key word about the uncanniness of the ordinary is *become*. I think of you and two seconds later the phone rings and there you are. In college I had a tutorial on Monday afternoons; on eleven consecutive Mondays, it rained. (I'm not making that up.)

Or consider acousmatic sound—sound from an unseen source.[2] It is perfectly commonplace. I hear you in the next room and know what you're doing. I wake up to the sound of birdsong outside my window. Acousmatic sound becomes fascinating only when it draws our attention away from the concerns of the moment. It becomes uncanny only when its invisibility is somehow wrong, inappropriate, inexplicable. It disturbs our equilibrium when it is sound we *should not* be hearing.

In Arthur Conan Doyle's "The Japanned Box" (the 1899 story discussed in entry 21, and also one of Toop's examples), the recorded voice on which the narrative turns is acousmatic at first. The narrator recalls hearing it years earlier when he tutored the sons of the widower who secretes the phonograph, "squat and uncouth," in the japanned box of the title.[3] (The toad-like ugliness of the machine recalls the fairy tale; when the husband aurally "kisses" the machine, it revives his wife's voice as if it were still a living woman's.) Returning home at night, the narrator had been surprised by a voice heard through an open window: "It was a voice—the voice undoubtedly of a woman. It was low—so low that it was only in that still night air that we could have heard it, but, hushed as it was, there was no mistaking its feminine timbre. It spoke hurriedly, gaspingly for a few sentences, and then was silent—a piteous, breathless, imploring sort of voice."[4] The narrator's employer had once been an infamous seducer, and the voice suggests he has resumed his old ways, though there is no apparent way the woman heard speaking so imploringly could get in the house without being noticed by the staff. But yes, there is, only not in the flesh. It turns out that the husband had been faithful to his wife and remains so to her voice. The voice's strangeness is the mark of mortal illness, which the phonograph endows with an uncanny life.

This solution is ironic. Doyle had a longstanding interest in spiritualism, which intensified greatly after the death of his son in World War I and of his brother and two nephews shortly afterward. From the point of view of the elder Doyle, hearing a dead person's voice would not be uncanny at all. But the source of uncanniness in the story is not spectral; it is technological. At the time of the incident the phonograph was too new. It simply never occurred to the tutor that the voice he overheard might be mechanically reproduced. Hence his bemusement.

44 The Contralto Mystique

INTERCESSION

Between roughly the 1820s and the 1920s, the contralto voice, the rarest of all voice types, enjoyed a transcendental mystique. Traces of its elevation, linked to its rarity, persist into the present, as does the descriptive language that the voice attracts. A recurrent trope is the supposed vanishing of the true contralto; the phrase "true contralto" is itself an accolade. Writing on the centenary of the birth of Kathleen Ferrier (1912–53), Tom Huizenga illustrates the persistence of the metaphor, with a hint of the gender fluidity that will be part of our concern: "Her voice was a true contralto, radiant and rich with velvety purple tones reaching deep into a manly range."[1]

Johannes Brahms's "Alto Rhapsody" (1869), a setting for contralto, male chorus, and orchestra of some verses by Goethe, is widely admired, but virtually no one has asked the seemingly obvious question of why Brahms wrote it for contralto. The poetry, an excerpt from Goethe's "Harz Journey in Winter" (1777), describes the plight of a self-tormenting misanthrope as he wanders "apart" in the Harz mountains, losing his way until "the emptiness engulfs him" (or devours him: *die Öde verschlingt ihn*). After a period of reflection, the narrator pleads with the "Father of love" to quicken the wanderer's heart; the choice of verb echoes the twenty-third Psalm in Luther's German translation. Brahms stops there, well before Goethe's narrator dissolves the distinction between the wanderer and himself. Just so: himself. The wanderer is—always has been—his alter ego. So why the contralto? Why the dusky timbre of the voice? Why change the sex of the narrator? Just who is speaking here, and for whom?[2]

Could the narrator in the rhapsody be the wanderer's beloved? There is a biographical story that might suggest as much. Brahms seems to have fallen in love with Julie Schumann, one of Robert and Clara Schumann's daughters, and to have composed the piece shortly after being virtually traumatized by the announcement of her engagement to an Italian count. But even allowing for the personal element, the music has other ideas. Beloveds are sopranos. Thinking of opera, the most famous contralto role in Brahms's day was that of Orpheus in Christoph Willibald Gluck's *Orpheus and Eurydice* (1762). The lost beloved is, correspondingly, a soprano. Besides, the wanderer, unlike Orpheus, is alienated from all humanity. As the saying goes, he is someone only his mother could love.

And that, emotively if not conceptually, is the case here. The "Alto Rhapsody" is music of solicitude—a rarity, like the voice. The work begins with maternal empathy after a searing orchestral prelude; it evolves by gaining psychological insight into the wanderer's predicament; and it ends with an intercession on his behalf. The outcome, strictly speaking, remains unknown. The concluding plea is pointedly conditional: "*If*, on your psaltery, / Father of love, there is one note / his ear can hear, / then quicken his heart!" (emphasis added).[3] At this point the music, turning from C minor to C major, becomes rhapsodic indeed. It takes on the task it asks the Father to perform. The music itself seeks the healing note and effectively grants its own prayer in the act of uttering it.

If the rhapsody really was provoked by the marriage of Julie Schumann (Brahms did present it to her as a wedding gift), the biographical element—the end of any hope of marriage for Brahms, and not just with Julie but with anyone—may reflect a turn to idealized mother love as a substitute. That would be consistent with the memorial impulse in Brahms's *German Requiem*, which was partly inspired by his mother's death and which he completed just a year before the "Alto Rhapsody."

The contralto voice would thus embody the earth's maternal lullaby.
And not for the first time, at least according to Friedrich Kittler, who finds
in the German world of the early nineteenth century a growing identifica-
tion of the mother's lullaby with both the emotional power of lyrical lan-
guage and the restorative power of nature. The low-voiced lullaby was at
once a nursery practice and an aesthetic ideal.[4] One of Kittler's illustra-
tions is a lyric by Clemens Brentano, who with Achim von Arnim edited
Des Knaben Wunderhorn (Youth's magic horn, 1805–8), a collection of
folk poems from which Gustav Mahler would draw texts for a dozen songs.
The language, especially in the first and last lines, grants its own plea
much as the rhapsody does:

> Singet leise, leise, leise,
> Singt eine flüsternd Wiegenlied . . .
> Wie die Bienen um die Linden
> summen, murmeln, flüstern, rieseln.

> Sing softly, softly, softly,
> Sing a whispering lullaby . . .
> Like the bees around the linden
> Hum, murmur, whisper, flutter.[5]

More broadly, the rhapsody contributes to the contralto mystique by mak-
ing explicit its endowment of the voice with a unique fusion of the sensory
and the numinous. In his 1824 biography of Rossini, the novelist known as
Stendhal wrote in praise of Giuditta Pasta that her voice, which could range
from contralto to soprano, was "not only very beautiful" but also possessed of
"a certain sonorous and magnetic vibration" that, for physical reasons still
unexplained, "grabs [*s'empare*]" the spirit of the listener with the rapidity of
lightning. In 1847, Henry Chorley described the voice of Marietta Alboni as
"a rich, deep, real *contralto*, of two octaves from G to G—as sweet as honey—
. . . and with that tremulous quality which reminds fanciful speculators of the
quiver in the air of the calm, blazing, summer's noon."[6]

Richard Wagner would channel the mystique to tragic ends in the fig-
ure of Erda, the all-knowing earth mother, who first appears in *Das
Rheingold*, a work finished, like the rhapsody, in 1869. Erda's contralto
voice enters late in the narrative and is unlike anything that precedes it.
Its dark timbre, ringing with prophesy, comes as no less a shock than the

apparition of Erda herself as she suddenly rises from the depths to con-
front Wotan. In productions that follow Wagner's stage directions,[7] we see
only the upper half of her body, obscured by a mysterious blue light; she is
there to be *heard*. Her voice is not just that of a "scolding woman [*mah-
nendes Weib*]," as Wotan calls her at first, but the voice of a Sibyl.

The ruination of the contralto across the span of the *Ring* measures the
inexorable ruin of the gods' world order. Although much depends upon
the production, both the libretto and the music of the *Ring* strongly sug-
gest that a steep decline in sibylline power occurs between *Das Rheingold*
and *Siegfried* and dwindles down to nothing in *Götterdämmerung*. Erda
in *Siegfried* is confused about her own prophecy and sings disjointedly.
Her haggard eldest daughter, the First Norn of *Götterdämmerung*, also a
contralto, knows only the past and loses her grasp of it as the rope of des-
tiny unravels in her hands. Before its final installment, the tragic form
depicts itself in the symbol that foretells its denouement.

Misfortune rather than tragedy shadows the title character of George
Eliot's verse play *Armgart* (1870). Armgart is a contralto who triumphs in
the iconic role of Gluck's Orpheus, as did her probable model, Eliot's
friend Pauline Viardot. (The role, first sung in 1762, was originally writ-
ten for castrato.) At its height Armgart's voice suggests Ceres as well as
Orpheus. It is revivifying, "like the summer sun / That ripens corn." When
she sang in the Gluck, "the house was held / As if a storm were listening
with delight / And hushed its thunder."[8] But Armgart is fated to lose her
voice irretrievably only a year later, with no one to intercede for it. In voice
she becomes the Eurydice to her own Orpheus. Her fate is doubly ironic
because the Orpheus of Gluck's opera, unlike the Orpheus of myth, suc-
ceeds in saving Eurydice in the end. The contralto voice, anticipating the
earthly burdens it would later assume, reaches its expressive peak in
Orpheus's lament when he thinks that Eurydice has been lost. The lament
is famously in a major key, more wistful than sorrowful and already inter-
ceding, albeit unknowingly, on its own behalf.

The mystique continues in Walt Whitman's prose vignette "A Contralto
Voice" (1880) and Thomas Hardy's poem "In a Museum" (ca. 1916):

In the evening air, the church-choir and organ on the corner . . . gave
Luther's hymn, *Ein feste Berg*, very finely. The air was borne by a rich con-

tralto. For nearly half an hour there in the dark . . . came the music, firm and unhurried, with long pauses. The full silver star-beams of Lyra rose silently over the church's dim roof-ridge. Varicolor'd lights from the stain'd glass windows broke through the tree-shadows. And under all—under the Northern Crown up there, and in the fresh breeze below, and the *chiaro-scuro* of the night, that liquid-full contralto.[9]

Here's the mould of a musical bird long passed from light,
Which over the earth before man came was winging;
There's a contralto voice I heard last night,
That lodges in me still with its sweet singing.

Such a dream is Time that the coo of this ancient bird
Has perished not, but is blent, or will be blending
Mid visionless wilds of space with the voice that I heard,
In the full-fugued song of the universe unending.

Whitman and Hardy directly position the sensory presence of earthly life over a contralto undertone—the undertone of all things. Whitman makes the voice the earthly counterpart of the constellations Lyra, the lyre, and the near-perfect semicircle of the neighboring Northern Crown. Hardy foretells the blending of two lost sounds, one he has never heard and one he has, in a cosmic chorus to come. Both hear the sound of the audiable as a distant contralto. Even close up the sound elicits awe, as Wagner reveals. It even moves Wotan to surrender the Ring, though at the cost of too much foreknowledge. The voice in its depth and rarity carries the sound of its own transience, and of the listener's. "Death," it says, antic-ipating Wallace Stevens in "Sunday Morning," "is the mother of beauty."[10]

William Styron bears witness to this relationship in his memoir of depression, *Darkness Visible.* He recalls being dissuaded from imminent suicide by a "soaring passage" from the "Alto Rhapsody"—it could only be the C-major plea—in a film he had forced himself to watch. The sound of the contralto voice, floating through a corridor from an unseen source, immediately quickens his heart (he uses the metaphor, though the quick-ening comes as a wound): "This sound, which like all music—indeed, like all pleasure—I had been numbly unresponsive to for months, pierced my heart like a dagger, and in a flood of swift recollection I thought of all the joys the house had known: the children who had rushed through its rooms, the festivals, the love and work. . . . All this I realized was more than I could ever abandon."[11]

Styron later realizes that the music's vivifying power had been literally maternal. It recalled the voice of his mother, Pauline, who died when he was thirteen. Pauline was a trained musician who loved the "Alto Rhapsody" and used to sing it around the house. (The family also owned a Victrola recording.)[12] But at first Styron hears none of this. The quickening precedes the memory; the music's maternal intercession moves him *before* it recalls the voice of his own mother. His decision not to die may have been "belated homage" to her: "In those last hours before I rescued myself, when I listened to the passage from the *Alto Rhapsody*—which I'd heard her sing—she had been very much on my mind."[13] His prior thoughts have no power to move him until the music's contralto voice intercedes and once again grants its own prayer.

But the maternal metaphor invokes a sense of security that it cannot sustain. Even Brahms admits as much with the *if* clause that begins the intercession of the rhapsody. Whitman and Hardy depersonalize the voice by diffusing it. Neither gives the singer an identity, let alone a name. Wagner presents Erda, even in *Das Rheingold,* as beyond categorization. She is not a god but not a mortal, authoritative but helpless, prescient but (in *Siegfried*) bewildered. Gustav Mahler subsequently moves the contralto voice to a similar, uncategorizable, in-between position. He does it more than once. Mahler is next.

45 The Contralto Mystique II

DEPARTURE

Of Mahler's eleven symphonic works—the nine complete symphonies, the incomplete tenth, and *Das Lied von der Erde*—five use voices, and, of these, three give special prominence to contralto solos. As with Brahms, virtually no one seems to have asked why. But as the preceding entry suggests, the earth holds the answer.

Mahler revisits the contralto voice in ways that tie together three needs felt to be elemental. There is the need for the deep, vivifying resonance imaged in Eliot's ripening corn and Stendhal's soul-seizing magnetism; the need for solicitude voiced in Brahms's "Alto Rhapsody"; and the need of life for sound. The sound that voices these needs must also be the sound that answers them. In the contralto movements of the Second and Third Symphonies and *Das Lied*, the voice is that of the earth, but not of mother earth. Mahler universalizes the voice to speak of human suffering and seek a path beyond it. The contralto is the voice of mortal life, earthly life, itself.

The speaker in "Urlicht" (Primal light), the text sung by the contralto in the penultimate movement of the Second Symphony, is probably a child and certainly childlike. The text's central struggle with a diminutive angel—*Engellein*, wee angel—points to a child's version of the biblical clash between Jacob and the angel of God who wrestles with him until dawn and breaks his hip.[1] The path to heaven is scaled down to a child's size. But the image introduced in the first line carries a subtext that has put away childish things:

O Röschen rot,
Der Mensch liegt in größter Not,
Der Mensch liegt in größter Pein,
Je lieber möcht' ich im Himmel sein.

O little red rose!
Man lies in greatest need!
Man lies in greatest pain!
I'd much rather be in heaven.[2]

The rose comes laden with age-old burdens—of transience, passion, sacrifice, and salvation—that the speaker can invoke but not grasp. But the contralto voice, here primal voice to match the primal light, grasps it all too well. She sings the words of the text to convey and console what the text cannot say: that the path to heaven does not lead away from need and pain but through them. Mahler sets the first line in isolation so that the rose remains both a simple sensory image and an enigma. In the religious context, the immediate point of symbolic reference is probably the Virgin,

one of whose titles is Rosa Mystica, the mystic rose, but at the same time
the rose is, yes, a rose.[3]

The anguish that the singing voice brings to the two interior lines is all
too laden with experience, as is the tortuous harmony beneath them. The
disparity persists throughout. The music of the song knows better than its
language, and it says so. The voice we hear is neither the child's nor the
adult's, the voice neither of innocence nor experience. It is vividly present
(the contralto timbre sees to that) but impossible to pin down.

The first thing we hear after the apostrophe to the rose is the sound of
the neither/nor. The gap between innocence and experience becomes
audible in a flaw found—implanted—in the parallel statements of greatest
need and greatest pain. The melodies for these statements are nearly iden-
tical, but their harmonies break the melodic parallel. They fashion the
melodies into a kind of Janus face. The voice, despite its caressing rich-
ness, becomes split within itself along a hairline fracture. The splitting
continues in the childlike "I'd much rather be in heaven." The statement is
doubled to balance the double statement of need and pain, but it is also
divided against itself—the melodies are no longer parallel—and in search
of a tonal resolution it does not find.[4]

Even more telling, perhaps, are the three exposed moments of voice
that punctuate the setting of the first three lines, like catches in the throat.
For the "O" that begins the movement and the "Der" of "Der Mensch" in
the lines about need and pain, the contralto sings unaccompanied. The
syllables are insignificant; the voice is anything but. Its solicitude is clear-
est when the voice is momentarily stripped bare. No matter who we hear,
what we hear is the contralto voice, still the voice of Orpheus, the voice of
intercession that changes the whole course of the symphony and opens the
gates to the symphony's choral finale.

·   ·   ·   ·   ·

The contralto returns in the Third Symphony to sing the "Midnight Song"
from Nietzsche's *Thus Spoke Zarathustra*. Here again the voice is neither
one thing nor another, in this case neither male nor female—a positive
neither/nor, not an equivocal both/and. The contralto's voice absorbs the

voice of Zarathustra into the higher-order voice of midnight itself—the actual speaker of these lines—to validate the judgment that, in the contest of woe and joy, joy is the deeper. Deeper, not because of what it has, but because of what it wants:

> O Man! Take heed! . . .
> Woe says: perish!
> But all joy wants eternity—,
> —wants deep, deep eternity![5]

The music ultimately finds what it wants in a moment of enhanced vocalization. After hewing throughout to a speechlike manner, with one note per syllable, the symphony's contralto voice suddenly presses forward to sound the depth—deeper than woe, deeper than sex—that the poem seeks. The voice frees itself to sing the two concluding lines in long-breathed, undulating, lyrical melody. The undulation dwells primarily on the word "tief," deep, literally absorbing the word and its meaning into the sound of the voice. Unlike its "soaring" counterpart in the "Alto Rhapsody," however, this deep-rooted contralto cannot grant its own desire in the act of expressing it. To do so would be to give itself the lie. The gap between wanting and being is still unbridged. But never mind. The wanting is what matters. Accordingly the melody comes fully to rest but the movement does not. Adrift on a solitary octave deep in the bass, the movement ends without resolution, knowingly seeking a future that may never arrive.

Even so, the contralto Zarathustra refuses the dark counsel of Wagner's seers. Erda and the First Norn embody the inexorable passage from joy to woe, the reverse but also the mirror image of the path taken by the voice in the "Alto Rhapsody." Mahler's symphonic movements follow Brahms, but they recast solace as aspiration and longing. *Das Lied* follows Wagner, but with a recurrent lyricism, often very delicate, that escapes (by just enough) the call of nihilism.

.   .   .   .   .

Das Lied von der Erde is a setting of six German adaptations of classical Chinese poems. It alternates between tenor (songs 1, 3, and 5) and contralto (songs 2, 4, and 6). The alto part may also be taken by a baritone, but the music was conceived for a very dark contralto, Sara Cahier, who was known for her Erda, recorded "Urlicht," and sang in the posthumous premiere of *Das Lied*. The two voices form an antithesis to the romantic pairing of tenor and soprano. They sing as if oblivious of each other, each voice clinging to its own vision of life. Mahler's title is precise in its ambiguity, borne out by what the voices convey. The tenor sings *about* the earth, especially about the woes he escapes with the joys of drink. The contralto sings *for* the earth and above all of earthly partings. The tenor frames a celebration of friendship with two drinking songs. The contralto frames a description of youthful pleasures with two mourning songs. The trajectories contradict each other, but they do not stand on equal terms. The contralto has the long last word. Its trajectory *corrects* the more superficial course of the tenor, even at the cost of accepting the miseries that the tenor prefers to drink away. But this voice has no sex, because the earth has none, and the contralto voice sounds like the song of the earth.

The voice even bears a trace of Nietzschean yea-saying, a dying echo of Zarathustra's "Midnight Song." By clinging to joy as it flies, the voice refuses the imperative to perish issued by its own woe. The echo is strongest in the final song, "Der Abschied," "The Farewell", where it extends to the contralto's parting words. Added by Mahler, along with a lyrical description of "the beloved earth," those words, famously, are "ewig . . . ewig . . . ," "forever . . . forever . . ." They are heard nine times, low in the contralto's rich middle register, before the last of them dies away *pianississimo*. And here too there is a positive neither/nor based on the contralto's dissolution of sex.

"Der Abschied" is nearly as long as the preceding five songs combined. It concerns the final parting of two old friends. Both are men. The movement—one can hardly call it a song—consists of two vocal halves separated by a long orchestral interlude. The texts of the vocal segments are presented as if to narrate a single farewell, but they are different poems by different poets. By coming between them, the interlude musically enacts the necessity of parting. But it also enacts the apotheosis of the contralto voice.

The opening poem is narrated in the first person present tense. When the contralto sings it, her neither/nor voice of the earth absorbs the voice of the speaker as, in "The Midnight Song," it absorbs the voice of

Zarathustra. Here too the depth of the voice is deeper than its sex. The contralto sings the speaker's farewell for him, or rather his longing to say farewell, since his friend has not yet arrived at their rendezvous. But the closing poem is narrated in the third person past tense. It begins with the word "He," already at the remove of the contralto in the "Alto Rhapsody." Its voice no longer speaks *as* one of the friends, but only *of* the friends. It no longer tells who they are but who they were. The voice comes home to itself by becoming no person's voice but only the voice—and the only voice—able to sing the song of the earth: the contralto voice that commiserates and endures.[6]

The breadth of "Der Abschied" immerses the listener in the passage of time, which, in the end, the music can barely bring itself to let go. The ninefold repetition of "ewig" is a way of buying time before eternity takes it away. The word is sung as a descending step reluctant to reach its second syllable. Its first two utterances are conjoined but the others are widely separated, as if to defer and defer again the moment when the singing has to stop. The lingering, a kind of slow rocking, makes the coming of that moment almost bearable. The contralto "ewig" becomes the refrain of the earth's no-longer-maternal lullaby. Its incessant repetition brings the word to the limits of its capacity to mean. At some indeterminate point it may even cease to be language. Its yea-saying passes little by little to the extraordinarily delicate web of instrumental sound spun round it, into which it ultimately fades. The "yes," in Wittgenstein's terms, can no longer be said, but only the auditory equivalent of shown.

Even that much affirmation would subsequently be lost along with the culture that made it possible. Karl Amadeus Hartmann's First Symphony, "Attempt at a Requiem" (begun in 1938 and completed in 1955), was composed with Brahms, Wagner, and Mahler surely in mind. The work is a reflection on the Nazi era and the catastrophe it wrought. So great a ruin leaves nothing behind but lamentation, rendering even mourning impossible—hence the "attempt" of the title, for which read "failed attempt." The final threnody, based, like the movements preceding it, on the poetry of Walt Whitman, is sung by the earth-identified figure that Whitman calls the Mother of All (for Hartmann, "die Allmutter"). She is, of course, a contralto, but one who is as much "apart there" and pathless as the wanderer of the "Alto Rhapsody." In "Attempt at a Requiem," accordingly, the orchestral style of "Der Abschied," alternately delicate and poignant, is swept away on waves of violent sound. But perhaps more consequential, though less overt, is the resexualization of the voice via the maternal metaphor. The Mother of All here does not speak *for* the earth, but *to* it—and for Hartmann, if not for Whitman, she speaks in vain.

This irretrievable farewell reveals the lesson of the contralto mystique more fully than its forerunners. The mystique is mostly a thing of the past. It has an afterlife in performances of the Brahms and Mahler and in recordings of legendary contraltos such as Ferrier and Marian Anderson. That it can do that much points to the need it once fulfilled, the pain it once relieved: to give sound itself a voice, and a voice more benign than the world.

46 Two Lynchings

The penultimate chapter of W. E. B. Du Bois's *The Souls of Black Folk* is a short story, "Of the Coming of John." The protagonist is one "John Jones," a Black everyman, as his name tells us, but the biblical ring of the title suggests another John, John the Baptist, whose fate prefigures his namesake's. John the Baptist has his head severed at the neck; John Jones is hanged by it. For the story ends, all too plausibly, with a lynching.

The lynching, however, is not described. Instead it is condensed into a single sentence, also a paragraph unto itself, with which the story ends: "And the world whistled in his ears." The sentence is enigmatic for several reasons. For one, it outruns time; it whips by in a rush. As the lynching party approaches, and a rider whose eyes "flash red with fury" bears the "coiling twisted rope," John closes his own eyes and, as if just in the blink of an eye, the reader's eye, the text skips to the moment of the hanging. The world whistling in John's ears is presumably the rush of air that accompanies, that envelops, his body as it is strung up or dropped down; either way it is the last sound he hears.

It is also the antithesis of another sound that has played a large role in John's life: the sound of Wagner's *Lohengrin* Prelude, heard at the

Metropolitan Opera on a trip to New York. Du Bois calls it the music of Lohengrin's swan, the symbol of a promised redemption that leads to tragedy. But the promise continues to echo as John waits to be lynched: long and smooth as opposed to the swift and sharp whistling air—a glide rather than a swipe. As John gazes into the distance, he hears this music again in his mind's ear, but with a vividness that suggests it is somehow actually present. But he also hears the music fuse with the noise that will obliterate it, the thundering hooves of his murderers: "Clear and high the faint sweet melody rose and fluttered like a living thing, so that the very earth trembled as with the tramp of horses and murmur of angry men. He leaned back and smiled toward the sea, whence rose the strange melody, away from the dark shadows where lay the noise of horses galloping, galloping on." In both its transcendental and its tragic aspects, John's destiny comes to him on tides of sound.[1]

Du Bois does not attempt, and perhaps in 1900 could not have published, anything like the graphic account of a lynching that James Baldwin gave in his "Going to Meet the Man" (1965).[2] But there are overlaps. In each case a racial alter ego plays a decisive role: in Du Bois it is the white former playmate and namesake who tries to rape John's sister, and in Baldwin it is the nameless Black man whose lynching the white protagonist had witnessed when a boy. (His parents had taken him to see the ordeal "like a Fourth of July picnic." The boy, who would grow up to be a brutal sheriff's deputy, screams at the exact moment when a knife castrates the victim, with whose penis he, the boy, is deeply preoccupied. A moment earlier he had felt his own scrotum tighten and then seen the victim looking him straight in the eye.) In Baldwin too music forms the antithesis of racial violence. In this case it is a spiritual, "I stepped in the river at Jordan," first heard by the boy while being driven "to meet the man." The song comes to the deputy "out of nowhere"; with it comes "an overwhelming fear, which yet contained a curious and dreadful pleasure." The memory of the lynching then comes rushing back in excruciating detail. Yet despite his horror at what he recalls, apparently for the first time, the traumatic memory only intensifies the boy-man's racism—on display earlier in the story when, in a futile effort to stop the sound of Black demonstrators singing, he beats a man nearly to death and, among other things, stabs at his victim's testicles with a cattle prod.

47 "White Christmas"

SAIGON, 1975

The 1942 movie musical *Holiday Inn*, which receives high audience rankings on Amazon Prime and Rotten Tomatoes, features a flimsy (actually rather repellant) romantic plot and a solid episode of blackface racism. But it also features Fred Astaire dancing to the music of Irving Berlin, and Bing Crosby singing Berlin songs, the best known of which is "White Christmas." Crosby's recording of that well-loved number became (and remains) the best-selling single ever made. One has to suppose that in 1942 it simply did not occur to anyone that the "white" in "White Christmas" might refer to something more than the color of snow. It does seem to have occurred to Irving Berlin, who cut the scene of blackface minstrelsy when the movie was remade in 1954. It may also have occurred to the U.S. Armed Forces Radio in 1975, unless they were as oblivious as the makers of *Holiday Inn*. Either way, as Ocean Vuong observes in the introductory note to his poem "Aubade with Burning City," they broadcast "White Christmas" as a code to begin the evacuation by helicopter of American civilians and Vietnamese refugees during the fall of Saigon on April 29, 1975. The city, Vuong's grandmother told him, "fell during the snow song."

"Aubade" belongs to a small but distinguished group of literary works that cannot be fully understood unless the reader knows how a certain piece of music sounds. In most cases the music is classical (usually German, preponderantly by Beethoven). Leo Tolstoy's novella "Family Happiness" depends on Beethoven's "Moonlight Sonata" as his infamous "The Kreutzer Sonata" depends on, well, the "Kreutzer" Sonata (Beethoven encore); Thomas Mann's novel *The Magic Mountain* ultimately pivots on Schubert's song "Der Lindenbaum" (The Linden Tree); James Fenton's poem "A German Requiem," a Holocaust elegy, depends on Brahms's choral work by that name, even though, unlike "Aubade," its text makes no reference to the music. But highly recognizable popular music can play the same role. Richard Flanagan's novel *The Sound of One Hand Clapping*, about refugee life in Tasmania in the decades after the Second World War, makes ironic, or perhaps nostalgic, use of "Lara's Theme" from the movie *Doctor Zhivago* while describing a world in which romantic love is a cruel joke. "Aubade" is a particularly vivid example of the genre because one simply has to sing "White Christmas" in one's head while reading; not to do so is not to read the poem at all. The underlying irony is the assumption that virtually any American reader can do that.

The poem begins with a mysterious image suggesting the difficulty of separating historical memory from fiction even when the underlying facts are undisputed:

> Milkflower petals on the street
> 　　　　　　　　like pieces of a girl's dress.
>
> *May your days be merry and bright . . .*[1]

Milkflower blooms in the fall, not in the spring, and in Hanoi, not in former Saigon. The milkflower petals cannot be literal, and we do not yet know that the image presented as figurative, the girl's dress, probably *is* literal. The only thing we can be sure of is the song. A collage of details follows. Prominent among them are traces of a romantic rendezvous involving a white dress (befitting the genre of the aubade, which recounts the parting at morning of usually illicit lovers), the metaphor of falling snow, and ironic juxtapositions of the idyllic "snow song" with the horrific details of the April day—a dead man face down in a pool of Coca-Cola, clutching a photograph of his father; a black dog with crushed hind legs; a Buddhist nun incinerating herself. It is possible to piece some of these details together into an exemplary narrative though impossible to verify the result. The mere possibility, the mere likelihood, is bad enough. But there is at least the strong suggestion that what parts the lovers is a blast that rips through the window of their hotel room, killing them and showering down fragments of the girl's white dress on the streets. The shreds of the dress form the unseasonable snow as the song "mov[es] through the city like a widow"—a widow who, following Vietnamese custom, would wear a white headband: white, of course, as snow.

The italicized song lyrics that punctuate the poem stand in self-mocking antithesis to the details recorded in roman type. But the deeper irony comes not from the contradiction between song and event, but from the realization that there is no contradiction; the event has always been there in the song. The violence of the event idles in the idyll of "White Christmas," biding its time. So, while American readers can sing the song in their heads while reading, and perhaps cannot help singing it, the gradual realization dawns, or should dawn, that they—we—*should not be doing this*. At that point the sound becomes unbearable.

48 The Ghetto

NEW YORK, 1904

Vuong writes from a dual perspective that is hard to inhabit. He is Vietnamese by birth but was born decades after the events recalled in his "Aubade with Burning City." They can be only history to him. But he was brought to the United States at age two; Vuong is an American, as culpably familiar with "White Christmas" as anyone else in the country. His situation, however, is not new, and neither is its sensitivity to sound.

When Henry James in 1904 returned to the United States after an absence of more than twenty years, he was both fascinated and distressed by the presence of the immigrant multitudes that had arrived in the meantime, especially in Manhattan, where he had spent his boyhood, and which was no longer—not even remotely—the city he had known then. His reflections on this change, published in his travel memoir *The American Scene,* are intricate, ambivalent, and extended. James—and of course this will sound familiar well over a century later—felt displaced by "the foreign" and "the alien," even though he knew very well that these feelings were unjust. "Who and what is an alien," he wrote, "when it comes to that, in a country peopled from the first under the jealous eye of history?—peopled, that is, by migrations at once extremely recent, perfectly traceable and urgently required. They are still, it would appear, urgently required—if we look about far enough for the urgency; though of that truth such a scene as New York may well make one doubt. Which is the American, by these scant measures?—which is *not* the alien . . . and where does one put a finger on the dividing line?"[1]

James struggled to reconcile his resentment and his sense of justice by fusing them into a feeling of fascination. He fails more often than he succeeds. He lets the struggle show on the page, oscillating, sometimes wildly, between close observation, abstract reflection, and ugly caricature. He indulges in circumlocution even more than usual for his labyrinthine late style. It is as if the sheer sound of his words, fantastically spun out, were his best means of defense against the predicament he recognizes while traveling on a crowded streetcar: that the "foreigner" feels just as much at home there as he does, perhaps more so, and is perfectly right to feel that way, whether James likes it or not. The eloquent, wide-spun web of Jamesian English becomes a kind of shibboleth—a term I use mindful of its Hebraic origin— that offers safe passage to the native speaker. This is a shibboleth for the mind's ear. The question is not can you say it, but can you *read* it.

The sound and the bustle of Jewish life on Manhattan's Lower East Side are the decisive forces in James's perplexity. They come together on a night spent absorbing the chorus of voices in the cafes and beer halls of the ghetto, one right after another. "That," he writes—and the passage requires extended quotation—

> That is where one's "lettered" anguish came in—in the turn of one's eye from face to face for some betrayal of a prehensile hook for the linguistic tradition as one had known it. Each warm lighted and supplied circle, each group of served tables and smoked pipes and fostered decencies and unprecedented accents, beneath the extravagant lamps, took on thus, for the brooding critic, a likeness to that terrible modernized and civilized room in the Tower of London, haunted by the shade of Guy Fawkes, which had more than once formed part of the scene of the critic's taking tea there. In this chamber of the present urbanities the wretched man had been stretched on the rack, and the critic's ear (how else should it have been a critic's?) could still always catch, in pauses of talk, the faint groan of his ghost. Just so the East side cafes—and increasingly as their place in the scale was higher—showed to my inner sense, beneath their bedizenment, as torture-rooms of the living idiom; the piteous gasp of which at the portent of lacerations to come could reach me in any drop of the surrounding Accent of the Future. The accent of the very ultimate future, in the States, may be destined to become the most beautiful on the globe and the very music of humanity (here the "ethnic" synthesis shrouds itself thicker than ever); but whatever we shall know it for, certainly, we shall not know it for English—in any sense for which there is an existing literary measure.[2]

Guy Fawkes aside (we will get to him momentarily), James writes in the accents, or say in the last "piteous gasp" of the accents, of the language he knows as English, English to the nth degree. The words and phrases and periodic sentences pile up like auditory barricades against a future accent that may, he admits, be both global and beautiful, but will not, alas, be his own. And of course he was right. He was right, at least, to predict, if not to regret, that the accent of the future could become, say, the accent (which is just an American accent) of Ocean Vuong, in a world where the lingua franca has become global English.

James's allusion to Guy Fawkes admits, perhaps unwillingly or unwittingly, to the unreasonableness of his fears. As any "English"—that is, British—reader would not need to be told, Guy Fawkes was a rebel who was caught on November 5, 1605, attempting to blow up Parliament with King James I in attendance. His capture is celebrated every November 5, a national holiday on which the "old Guy" is burned in effigy. James thus identifies the "living idiom" that he cherishes with the cries of a violent rebel tortured by the established order that he sought to overthrow.

The source of James's linguistic anguish was the sound of Yiddish, perhaps mixed with Yiddish-accented English replete with Yiddish words. As I recollect it from my own early childhood, in a family full of expert code switchers, the language was spoken with a great emphasis on its melodic fluidity, which does not go well with the more rhythmic character of spoken English. That fluidity may have intensified James's discomfort:

> The scene here bristled, at every step, with the signs and sounds, immitigable, unmistakable, of a Jewry that had burst all bounds. That it has burst all bounds in New York, almost any combination of figures or of objects taken at hazard sufficiently proclaims; but I remember how the rising waters, on this summer night, rose, to the imagination, even above the housetops and seemed to sound their murmur to the pale distant stars. It was as if we had been thus, in the crowded, hustled roadway, where multiplication, multiplication of everything, was the dominant note, at the bottom of some vast sallow aquarium in which innumerable fish, of over-developed proboscis, were to bump together, forever, amid heaped spoils of the sea.[3]

The water images in this passage are confused, signs that James's ambivalence has devolved into incoherence. The rising waters are a flood tide, the product of a modern Deluge in auditory form. Yet they are endowed with an almost involuntary lyricism; the hubbub dissipates into a murmur, like the sound of the sea in a shell, which is wafted to the stars. Then the waters grow still, reversing themselves into the contents of the murky ("sallow") aquarium with its anti-Semitic imagery of fish with big noses swarming amid sunken treasure—the last image retouching a particularly nasty slur with hints of nautical adventure and picturesque piracy. *Yo ho ho and a bottle of rum!* What a *mishigas* . . .

49 Testimony

A persistent theme in the poetry of Paul Celan, a Jew who survived the Holocaust but whose parents did not, is the difficulty of using language, especially German, to bear witness to the disaster. One possibility he considers is turning to music instead:

> *cello-entry*
> from behind pain:
> . . .
> two
> breath fire clouds
> dig in the book
> the noise in the temples opened,
>
> something becomes true . . .

> *cello-einsatz*
> von hinter dem Schmerz:
> . . .
> zwei
> Brandwolken Atem
> graben im Buch,
> das der Schläfenlärm aufschlug,
>
> etwas wird wahr . . .[1]

Although the music here is figurative, Celan intimates that its sound is still audible. The sound comes from behind language as it comes from behind pain. The something that becomes true does so in the ear of both the poem and the reader. The "breath fire clouds"—remembered traces of smoke from the crematoria—delve, dig, or grub in a book for something to set against the unspeakable. But their digging is a kind of gasping, and the book is a book of sounds, opened by a throbbing in the temples. The air is choked with the vocal debris exhaled into in the text.

By coming from behind pain, the cello-entry, in whatever medium we hear it, promises to add itself to the scene of remembrance and comprehend the incomprehensible. The sound of the cello entry is the something that is becoming true. But can any actual utterance bear that kind of truth? Can any music? (And keep in mind: It may also do the opposite. It may rally the faithful to murder. It may turn a killing spree into a festival. The innocence of music is a little-acknowledged myth.)

Another work of Holocaust testimony may offer some clues to an answer. In the opening segment of Claude Lanzmann's nine-hour Holocaust documentary *Shoah* (1985), a survivor of the death camp at Chelmno sings a Polish folk song. In doing so he gives the film the only kind of music its director would allow. Lanzmann had ruled out underscoring—music on the soundtrack without a source in the action. Underscoring was underlining, a superfluous emphasis that could only diminish the impact of the film's interviews with victims and perpetrators. Lanzmann wanted no glib humanizing of the inhuman, no false uplift of the kind that would later mar the documentary epilogue to Steven Spielberg's *Schindler's List,* in which Jews saved by Schindler parade by his grave wrapped in the warm halo of a pop chorale. But music is hard to banish. This one man sings; his name is Simon Srebnik; he sings a folk song. He sings it while boating on the same river where he had sung the same song as a death-camp inmate. One of only two survivors from Chelmno, he has lived to sing it because the Nazis liked his voice.

As the film begins we see Srebnik amid green trees and rushing water in medium-long shot. He is sitting quietly in a boat being carried upriver. The camera slowly tracks his progress. He begins to sing; after a moment the boat passes behind a cluster of three tree trunks, so that we lose sight of the source of the song. When the boat emerges, it has receded far enough into the distance that we can no longer make a visual connection between the song and the singer, although we still see the man in the boat and know he is the one singing. The music floats and hovers. It lingers briefly then grows more distant and fades out under the sound of off-screen voices. In the space of about a minute, the song has been transformed from an act of memory, a fragment of testimony, to diffuse sound without a visible source—underscore after all.

This music escapes everyone's control. It escapes Simon Srebnik's because when the song becomes underscore it is no longer his. This dispossession is something we can see as well as hear. The singer dwindles on the screen as the song detaches itself and fades. But it also escapes Lanzmann's control. Attached to a scene of flowing water and pastoral woods, matched with camera movement that is lyrical in spite of itself, the song becomes beautiful and consoling. That we should know better does not matter. The song upends the refusal of a falsely emotive soundtrack. (As if in recoil, Lanzmann follows this shot immediately by returning the song to Srebnik, showing him in close-up as he sings again.) And finally the song escapes the viewer's control. It still remains an echo of the atrocities to which it testifies. The echo haunts the scene even as the song's loss of testimonial force continues. This song says too much, too much by far.[2]

Yet it is precisely in this excess that the song voices something about genocide on the terms set by Celan. The music becomes a sensory piece of memory, capable, like all melody, of unlimited repetition. It becomes a medium of survival, not so much for the singer who lived as for all those who died. The disembodied music floating over the river cannot be killed or corrupted. It absorbs and reciprocates the serene, detached beauty of the scene. And it does so not to deny but to affirm the irony that the occasion of its singing is the singer's return to the now-empty field where the killing apparatus once stood.

The end of the episode carries both the beauty and the irony a step further. The concluding image is a panorama of the lush pastoral landscape in which the flow of melody almost—*almost*—counterbalances the weight of irony. To reach this vantage point, the boat reverses course and passes downriver. Shown first in the middle distance, then as a decreasingly visible form in long shot, the boat and its passengers blend almost indistinguishably into the scenery. As that happens a voice-over nearly blots out the melody. These disappearances have more symbolic than testimonial value. For although the song and the singer remain separated (Srebnik is too far away to be seen singing), the song is different. It is not a Polish folk song but a German one. If it forms, to echo Celan, a voice entry, it hardly comes from behind pain. Its most prominent feature is a jolly refrain on the word *Warum*—Why?

50 Voice

It's a strange story when you think about it. A boy is spared from mass extermination because his captors like his voice. But some voices are like that. We just want to hear them. They address us not as the first and foremost conveyors of language but as sound: uniquely alluring or compelling sound. Everyday speech depends on a certain forgetting of sound. The primacy of language obscures the sensory side of speaking voice. Intonation takes second place to the word. We mostly hear changes of inflection as changes of meaning. When I make a vow or take an oath—when I give my word—it does not matter if my voice is agreeable, only that it is my voice.[1] But when voice becomes eloquent, when its timbre surpasses its language, it momentarily becomes paramount. Voice as sound is captivating. Preachers know that; demagogues know it; singers dream of it. One reason why radio has continued to thrive in a crowded media environment is that its invisibility magnifies the transient primacy of voice as sound. Franklin Roosevelt knew that; so did Hitler.

It is not too much of an exaggeration to say that the modern entertainment industry was born of the power of voice to become an object of desire. We don't know what Jenny Lind, the nineteenth century's Taylor Swift, sounded like, only that untold numbers of people flocked to swoon at her voice. But early recordings grew up with Caruso and the rest is media history, with its recurrent peaks of fan devotion or fan frenzy: Bessie Smith, Bing Crosby, Frank Sinatra, Billie Holiday, Nat King Cole, Maria Callas, Whitney Houston, Luciano Pavarotti—the list could go on and on. The temptation is just to recite the names, as if their sound too had a share of vocal charisma. Recording technology made it possible to compile an archive of charismatic voices. Even a speaking voice could be rescued from oblivion in the form of its sound. If we could still hear

Lincoln recite the Gettysburg address, it would not be the words that mat-tered. Anyone interested would surely know the words; many generations of Americans, mine included, would even have memorized them in school. What mattered would be the sound of his voice.

51 Inner Speech

Whose is the voice you hear in your head while you read? Whose but your own? But not your speaking voice; this is the voice that only you can hear. You only, unless . . . The voice in your head is yours when you read neu-trally, as when reading a newspaper or a text message. But the pleasure, and the value, of "reading"—there is no frigate like a book, said Emily Dickinson—is the transformation of your inner voice. One way to define "literature" is as writing designed to make you hear the voice in your head as (also) the voice of someone else, to hear your inner voice becoming another voice, another's voice.

For that to happen, something must impede your ability to read neu-trally, and it must happen in the text—or to the text—you're reading. Its language has to become "a kind of foreign language," as Marcel Proust put it, but a foreign language that you do not "know" yet somehow under-stand, at least a little. Gilles Deleuze, taking his cue from Proust, says that writers of literature "invent a new language within language. . . . They bring to light new grammatical or syntactic powers. They force language outside its customary furrows."[1]

Deleuze's specification of grammar and syntax offers a cue of its own. It situates the work of literature at the level, not of "style," but of the primary means by which language organizes itself, means that go unremarked in neutral reading. Language becomes literature by extrapolation, extension, amplification, drawing out the potentialities inherent in its formation of sentences. The metaphor of making unaccustomed furrows revives an age-old identification of writing, inscription, with the turning of a plow; only hard labor makes language fertile, but once harvested the ground must be left fallow before it can be plowed again.

How does this happen? The answer depends partly on the written medium, and partly on the caution that it does not follow a cause-and-effect sequence. Although the event of literature must occur within the text, the state of the text is not sufficient; the text has to be both written as literature (though that can happen accidentally or belatedly) and be read as literature. On the reading side, this begins with pace: although we do not always read by mentally rehearsing sentences, although we can take in sentences or even whole paragraphs at a glance, literature does its work for us only if we read slowly enough to hear, mentally, what we are reading, or even more slowly than that, not only to hear, but to listen. On the writing side, the work of literature goes differently depending on whether its medium is prose or poetry, the latter the older, ancestral form. Poetry thickens and formalizes language, filtering grammar and syntax through rhyme, meter, and lineation. Literary prose draws language out to form a continuous undulating flow of utterance. Poetry works by performative reading; prose works by immersion. (Exceptions duly noted.) They have in common, however, the recurrence of certain verbal traits that act as marks of the author's voice—and I do mean the author's, not the literary character's, though authors can give their characters the same kind of voice marks. These marks diffuse their effect over the text as a whole. They reverberate.

But all this is still not enough. The reader must make an affirmative contribution by becoming a willing surrogate, mentally lending a voice as well as an ear, emptying part of the self to accommodate the influx of the other. This is not easy to do. It requires a certain self-discipline, a certain forgetfulness of one's own condition. It is a skill seeking to feel like an instinct. It is a kind of acting in the theater of the text in which, as actor, one knowingly gets carried away by one's part.

52 The Deafness of Narcissus

Around 1597–1599, Caravaggio made a painting of Narcissus (figure 3).[1] It is an image of modernity, not of antiquity. Its subject is an elegantly

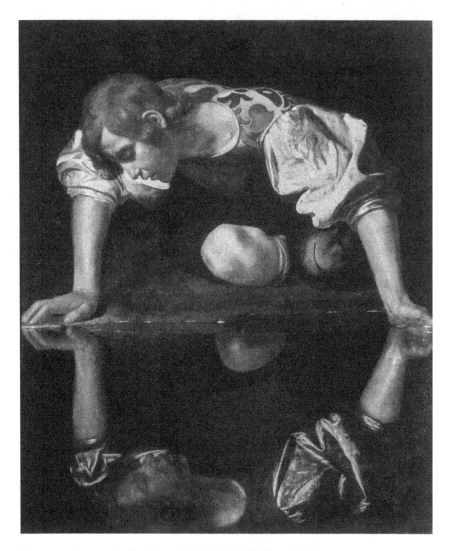

Figure 3. Caravaggio, *Narcissus* (1597–1599). Wikimedia Commons.

dressed young man of the painter's own day. He fills the picture space, which is without landscape (the background is black) and without Echo. The canvas is evenly divided top to bottom. The top half shows the youth in profile, leaning on his arms while staring down at his image in the pool, also black, a Stygian mirror. The bottom half shows the image staring up, its arms matching Narcissus's own to form a circle of reflection in which both are trapped. But the image is dark and indistinct; we can see in it what Narcissus cannot, that it absorbs his gaze while giving nothing back. In that sense it is the truest of reflections: Narcissus is he who absorbs the gaze and gives nothing back, not to Echo and not to the viewer.

The picture is strangely silent. All paintings are that, of course, but some give the impression of imaginary sound and some do not. Emphatically this one does not. Narcissus is not only blinded by his own gaze; he is deafened by it. In Ovid's *Metamorphoses,* where the story of Echo and Narcissus apparently originates, Narcissus rejects Echo as she repeats fragments of his own speech to him; cursed by Juno, that is all she can do. But Caravaggio's Narcissus is oblivious of Echo, who, again, is neither pictured nor alluded to. He simply cannot hear her.

Why not? One possibility is that Echo's multiplication of voice embodies a multiplication of desire that Narcissus, entranced by the youth in the pool, wants to avoid.[2] Another is that Echo's desire is an all-too-singular, all-too-accurate mirror of his own. Narcissus spurns Echo out of a hopeless love for the visual equivalent of an echo. He cannot untangle the mixture of recognition and projection found in any and every image of the one we desire, which is as close as we ever come to that elusive other. If Narcissus had only known what an echo is, he would not have fallen victim to one just because it appealed to his eye and not his ear.

That very ear may be the true subject of Caravaggio's painting. It appears—at eye level—as a kind of illuminated half-moon shining out amid the dark brown of Narcissus's hair. In contrast, Narcissus's eye is invisible, obscured by masklike shading; we can see his gaze blinding itself to reality. The image in the pool reproduces the masked eye but not the ear, which seems to have sunk into the depths of the pool. The missing ear is the invisible mark of an amputated hearing. The circle formed by the real and mirrored arms is an image not only of Narcissus's self-absorption but also of the silence that imprisons him. Outside the circle of speech, Narcissus falls into the circle of self-nullification. Like his model in Ovid, he is undone because his image, unlike Echo, cannot answer him, even in his own words.

When Lucian Freud in 1948 was asked to illustrate the myth of Narcissus, he did so by reconfiguring Caravaggio's painting.[3] His pen and ink drawing is also split into top and bottom halves, in this case unequal halves. But the image consists of nothing but a close-up of Narcissus propping up his face on his hands. He may be looking at nothing. We certainly can't tell if his eyes, veiled by their lashes, are gazing into the pool. The inverted image at the bottom of the drawing stops before reaching the eyes, as well it might; for this Narcissus, the gaze is secondary at best. Freud's Narcissus is even more profoundly deaf than Caravaggio's. His hands, grotesquely large, cover up his ears. In doing so they summon up another ancestor, the figure in the foreground of Edvard Munch's *The Scream* (not yet to be seen on coffee mugs and T-shirts). But where Munch shows a wide-open mouth, Freud draws one shut tight. His Narcissus utters nothing and hears nothing. Not yet dead, he is devoid of life because devoid of sound.

53 Sound in the Making

Performance in the arts depends on sound. The only exception, mime, is defined by the lack of sound; as always, the exception proves the rule. Until the early twentieth century, performance meant live performance, the only kind then possible. Its sound was sound in the making. Theaters and concert halls were resonators; some of them still are. Early cinema still depended on accompaniment by live music from the piano or, in the grander urban movie palaces, the organ or even the orchestra. But technology intervened. For over a century now the difference between live and fabricated performance has been the difference between plain and engineered sound. Real-time performance with elaborate sound design is more akin to recording than it is to live presence. Sound in the making by a live performer is what makes live performance *feel* alive.

This feeling is perhaps stronger in musical performance than it is in drama for the simple reason that in music, sound is the end as well as the means. Live music seems to address you in person much as someone telling you a story does, especially if the story has been told, or the music heard, before. Although the course of the narrative is familiar in general, each live iteration of it becomes something new and unexpected because it can always have been said differently, or badly, or not at all. Musical performance lives and thrives on those possibilities. More than storytelling, more than drama, it faces the ever-present risk of going bad or breaking down. The risk is meant to be embraced, not avoided. The vulnerability of music in performance is basic to its power as art. I like to think that this is especially true of classical music, which asks to be recreated in detail but also reinterpreted, but it is surely true of music in any genre. It remains true in drama as well, but less acutely there for at least two reasons. First, a dramatic action is to some degree independent of its realization, whereas the musical event is identical with its realization. Second, whereas human agency is plural in most drama, music presents itself as singular even when one is listening to an orchestra. Live music is thus the main heir of oral storytelling.

This inheritance is a historical development as well as an analogy. In his essay "The Storyteller" (1936), Walter Benjamin famously lamented the decline of oral storytelling that coincided with the rise of the modern novel. For Benjamin, "the novel" would not be oral even if it were read aloud. Other forms of printed narrative preserve traces of oral performance. The novel erases them:

> What differentiates the novel from all other forms of prose literature—the fairy tale, the legend, even the novella—is that it neither comes from oral tradition nor goes into it. This distinguishes it from storytelling in particular. The storyteller takes what he tells from experience—his own or that reported by others. And he in turn makes it the experience of those who are listening to his tale. The novelist has isolated himself. The birthplace of the novel is the solitary individual, who is no longer able to express himself by giving examples of his most important concerns, is himself uncounseled, and cannot counsel others.[1]

(I sometimes think that by "the novel" Benjamin simply means "Proust." Too bad he didn't pay more attention to modernist novelists in English. Woolf, Joyce, and Faulkner would certainly have set him straight about orality, though they would probably have agreed with him about counsel.)

Although Benjamin's argument exemplifies the regret for loss of immediacy that accompanies every new communications medium, every new technology of perception, it remains true that oral storytelling changed in (or out) of step with changes in communications technology. Its original form has endured primarily in the practice of reading or telling stories to young children. In the early twentieth century it migrated from in-person venues to live radio drama, then shifted briefly at mid-century to the next new medium, television, which relied heavily on live broadcasting for about a decade. But technology again intervened and television became primarily a recording medium. More recently, audiobooks and podcasts have found large audiences, but of course they are not live. Their popularity nonetheless testifies that even the illusion of storytelling in the present—live storytelling—has a utopian dimension that is not merely one among others. Storytelling still does what Benjamin says it used to do; it "gives counsel" to the community that gathers to hear it. But the best way to hear it may now be to go to a concert. It does not matter if the music does not tell a story; the music *is* the story. Provided it stays live enough, music in performance can assume the mantle of the storyteller. The modernization of art left gaps in oral storytelling. Live music offers to fill them.

Stories and storytelling are widely celebrated nowadays, almost as cheap replacements for higher-order systems of belief and value. A good story makes up for lost certainties. But the celebration is incomplete, and indeed unconvincing, without the element of liveness. Liveness undergirds the larger role of story in the social life of subjectivity: tell me your story, confess your secret, account for yourself, reveal yourself to me. This is the stuff of therapy, intimacy, drama, opera, and the news cycle.

The notion of narrative as cognition, social glue, and even neurocognitive mapping is now well established, almost to the point of needing to be questioned to avoid becoming a truism. As Benjamin's duality insists, storytelling is not the same thing as narrative, and of the two, it is storytelling that stands at the root of experience. Storytelling is not simply a form of knowing and sharing but a way of traveling, a kind of traveling in place. To experience storytelling is to place a stretch of time in a frame and to go through it willingly, with a certain self-surrender. It is to bear the concerns of the story—that is, to carry them and to endure them—as one's own. Narrative takes this experience of traversal as one element in a wider process; storytelling abandons itself to it.

Of course most music nowadays is recorded; recorded music is ubiquitous. But music in live (really live) performance can recapture the power

of storytelling, not despite the proliferation of other musical delivery sys-
tems, but as a consequence of them. When music becomes identified with
the event of its performance, it becomes more of what it has always been:
a means of experience that is immediate and intelligible at once. The
music incorporates not only the feeling of telling a story but also the con-
dition of vulnerability, strangeness, and openness that makes any story
matter. In live performance, but only there, the music's contribution to
storytelling is the virtual eruption of the life that animates it.

54 Housewarming

On November 18, 2000, the artist Anna Schuleit unveiled a one-day-only
sound installation at the ruins of the Northampton (Massachusetts) State
Hospital, a notoriously cruel mental asylum closed in 1993 after a long
legal struggle. The most notorious of the hospital's buildings, abandoned
in 1986, was known as the Old Main. Schuleit turned it into a loudspeaker
to broadcast one thing, one time, over the hospital grounds: a recording of
J. S. Bach's alternately festive and lyrical Magnificat for chorus and
baroque orchestra. Schuleit made a film of the event and later described
its genesis to an audience at the live storytelling series The Moth.[1]

The music affirms everything that the hospital denied. It is not clear
how many of the people in attendance were familiar with Bach in general
or with his Magnificat in particular or with the liturgical tradition of the
Magnificat, let alone its Latin text. What *is* clear is that none of that mat-
tered in the least. What did matter is that the ruined building, formerly a
scene of confinement, suffering, and hopelessness, became for half an
hour something like a gigantic gramophone horn from which the sounds
of voices and instruments burst out together, setting themselves free on
waves of jubilant song. Solo song could not have accomplished that; to
answer the suffering of many required the voices of many. It also required
that the technological apparatus be hidden from those on the scene,
though of course they knew it was there. For those present it should seem
as if the building had somehow been flooded by music out of nowhere and

was now in full overflow. The event should require suspension of disbelief; it should look and sound impossible.

The video, however, does show glimpses of the apparatus in the building's interior, as if to acknowledge that the structure, the ruin, would go on standing for some time after the music was over and the audience gone. (It was finally demolished in 2006.) The video's reaction shots are strongly affirmative but necessarily transient; the shots of the facade show the persistence of its decay in the midst of its passing transformation. The role of the music is not to obscure or "transcend" the cruel history of the place but to remember it and to be jubilant anyway.

Thomas Hardy's poem "The House of Silence" (ca. 1916) fills its own abandoned house with music to just the same end. But the key word here may be *silence:*

> "That is a quiet place—
> That house in the trees with the shady lawn."
> "—If, child, you knew what there goes on
> You would not call it a quiet place.
> Why, a phantom abides there, the last of its race,
>   And a brain spins there till dawn."
>
> "But I see nobody there,—
> Nobody moves about the green,
> Or wanders the heavy trees between."
> "—Ah, that's because you do not bear
> The visioning powers of souls who dare
>   To pierce the material screen.
>
> "Morning, noon, and night,
> Mid those funereal shades that seem
> The uncanny scenery of a dream,
> Figures dance to a mind with sight,
> And music and laughter like floods of light
>   Make all the precincts gleam.
>
> "It is a poet's bower,
> Through which there pass, in fleet arrays,
> Long teams of all the years and days,
> Of joys and sorrows, of earth and heaven,
> That meet mankind in its ages seven,
>   An aion in an hour."

Here too music awakens a dead house to life and overflows from indoors to out, this time enriched by the sound of laughter. The sound imparts vibrancy to the scene as bright light would impart luminousness. Or does it? The poem is cast as a dialogue between an elderly speaker who hears the music—for whom the whole scene is more lifelike than dreamlike—and a child who doubts him. It is by no means certain that the child's skepticism is wrong. The speaker candidly takes as real the music and dancing that he imagines, remembers, and longs for. But he does so as part of his poetic vocation. He may only be speaking metaphorically. It is impossible to be sure.

The last two lines encapsulate the dilemma. They contain contrary poetic allusions, as if the speaker's vocation were at war with itself. The closing line alludes to William Blake's "Auguries of Innocence," which urges its reader to "Hold Infinity in the palm of your hand / And Eternity in an hour." But the penultimate line recalls the famous "seven ages of man" speech from Shakespeare's *As You Like It*, which, to put it mildly, comes to a bad end:

> Last scene of all,
> That ends this strange eventful history,
> Is second childishness and mere oblivion;
> Sans teeth, sans eyes, sans taste, sans everything.[2]

55 Language Dead or Alive

Desire in the flesh was the great nemesis of St. Augustine, but desire in language was something else again. At one point in his book on the Trinity, Augustine forms syllabic sound, desire, and language into a trinity of their own. The bond joining these terms is more than merely practical. It seems, in securing the intelligibility of the word, to secure the intelligibility of the Word. It forms a fragment of the Incarnation at the root of the Trinity. Even everyday words have a latent sacramental character.

But more is involved than this word or that. Our desire to know the word, the desire of the word, carries over into the discourses that words form. This extension or, better, this overflow of our desire to the level of discourse is the basis of our absorption in what language says or evokes or narrates or explains. At its height, it produces an intoxication of/with language that includes rhythm and phonetic play and intonation as well as words. This rapture, whether written or spoken, is both a charm and a curse. It can draw us into its bedazzlement or deny us entry. Or both.

Augustine's ultimate concern is love for God, which the desire of the word serves to model. But the model has linguistic value independent of its doctrinal usage. Augustine identifies understanding a word with a combination of two factors: the sound of the spoken word apart from its meaning, and the fulfillment of a positive desire to know what the sound means. The unknown sound renders the voice "empty." Knowing the sign fills the gap. One passes from sound through desire to the sign.

Everyday language use obscures this dynamic because the everyday meaning of words is familiar. To bring out the underlying action one needs to consider a situation in which the familiar is put out of action. One might say that the aim of the literary text is to do just that; literature restores the desire of the word. It edges discourse toward the intoxication of language and brings us face to face with it. But Augustine tends to focus on elementals and accordingly works at the level of the word. The word for him (this man of many words) is a microcosm.

Augustine asks what it is like to encounter a word that is obsolete, like a word in a dead language. The disused word, we might say, is a dead spot in the living language. Augustine's Latin example, *temetum* (wine—an interesting choice, theologically speaking), is rich in sound, with its three alliterative syllables and the striking phonetic arch, *t-m-t*. A word such as this does the work of separating sound and meaning for us. At the same time it exposes the persistence of the desire it elicits: "The more the word is known, but not fully known, the more the mind desires accordingly to know what remains to be known."[1]

As befits a thinker for whom the body is a problem, Augustine presents the fulfillment of this desire as an irreversible progression, almost a spiritual progression: once we rise to the level of meaning, sound sinks below the threshold of concern. That, however, is just what it never does. When the empty voice becomes a full voice, the sound of the voice remains to be reckoned with. How the word is uttered is more often than not as germane as the word itself. So is the experience that the desired residue of knowledge is never exhausted, never fully claimed, but instead sustained by the sound that carries it as something further to be desired. Expression in language does not, because it cannot, stop with words.

This becomes all the more true when one expands the paradigm, first to include words that one does understand but finds puzzling or baffling in a particular usage, and then to include not just a word or sentence but an entire discourse, which repeats the dynamic on a larger, even more engrossing canvas. Hence the intoxication, the revelry of language in its own desire not only to mean but also to play with meaning and to dally with both nonsense and non-sense in an endless speech act.

Gerard Manley Hopkins's poem "The Wreck of the *Deutschland*," an elegy for five nuns drowned in a shipwreck, takes the desire of the word as its turning point in terms that Augustine might have appreciated. The poem takes the revelry of language as its premise. From the midst of it, Hopkins, as speaker, asks what one of the nuns meant by crying out "O Christ, Christ, come quickly!" After reviewing and rejecting several possible meanings, he exposes the gap left by the empty voice by taking it into his own speech. At a loss for words, he enjoins someone—the reader? Fancy (imagination) personified? Christ?—to give him, hand to him, the words he needs to keep the poem going:

> Other, I gather, in measure her mind's
> Burden, in wind's burly and beat of endragonèd seas.

> But how shall I . . . make me room there:
> Reach me a . . . Fancy, come faster—
> Strike you the sight of it? look at it loom there,
> Thing that she . . . there then![2]

The rest of the poem is a rhapsody on the "there then!," the sought-for meaning grasped as a sight and realized in waves of sound. That sound, rich in intonation, phonetic play, tortuous grammar, exclamations, bursts of consonants striking each other, and words scored with multiple meanings ("burden" as cross to bear, task to accomplish, and melody to sing in connection with one meaning of "measure") makes the desired meaning apparent but also exceeds it. The answer to Hopkins's plea comes less *in* his language then *as* his language.

The desire of the word does not often carry language as far as Hopkins takes it here, but the example, like Augustine's, embodies a more general pattern. To answer our desire to know, if not quite to satisfy it, language must sometimes break down in order to break through. Its burden is to rise from its own ashes. Or, as James Joyce measured the matter out from an even further extreme, "If you spun your yarns to him on the swish-barque waves I was spelling my yearns to her over cottage cake. . . . It's Phoenix, dear. And the flame is, hear!"[3]

56 Hearing Plato's Cave

Caves are full of echoes. Light there is sparse. When Plato constructed his allegory of the cave in book 7 of the *Republic,* he reversed these conditions. The cave where people in chains see only shadows on the wall and mistake them for reality is not dark. It is backlit by a great fire. The fire is not, of course, as bright as the sunlight outside, which remains unseen and unknown, but it is bright enough to cast the shadows. Between the fire and the prisoners' backs a procession of carriers passes, holding up artifacts to be projected along with the carriers' upper bodies. Plato's exposition of the allegory he builds up around this antique cinema is highly visual. Sight is paramount. Sound comes in as a kind of afterthought and the text abandons it soon after introducing it. Vision predictably dominates most commentary on the narrative—the scene—for what seems like good reason.

But perhaps we should listen more closely. The carriers make no attempt to hide their presence. They remain unseen but not unheard. Some are silent but some are talking. Plato, having observed this fact in passing, brings it back at a pivotal moment:

SOCRATES: If [the prisoners] could engage in discussion with one another, don't you think they would assume that the words they used applied to the things they see passing in front of them?

GLAUCON: They would have to.

SOCRATES: What if their prison also had an echo from the wall facing them? When one of the carriers passing along the wall spoke, do you

think [the prisoners] would believe that anything other than the
shadow passing in front of them was speaking?

GLAUCON: I do not, by Zeus.

SOCRATES: All in all, then, what the prisoners would take for true reality is
nothing other than the shadows of those artifacts.[1]

The prisoners make two errors about the sound of words. The first is to
assume that the words they speak refer to real things rather than to shad-
ows of them. The second is to believe that the words they hear are spoken
by the shadows they mistake for real persons. They hear echoes as voices.
In the order of Plato's exposition, vision comes first, but the error in vision
is confirmed by the errors in hearing. The prisoners' illusion cannot take
hold until it becomes embedded in speech. Speech accordingly becomes
the pivot by which Plato's argument arrives at its essential point: that
what the prisoners take for true and real is fictitious and artificial. In try-
ing to speak the truth, the prisoners just tell stories. Without knowing it
they resemble the puppeteers to whose shows Plato likens the procession
of artifacts.

But surely there is a performative contradiction here. If Plato, speaking
through Socrates, is right, then how can we trust him? His allegory, his
dialogue—all of his dialogues—are supposed to have their origin in speech.
If speech, and more particularly the exchange of speech, is fundamentally
mistaken about its object, then it has no access to truth. Worse yet, the
dialogues can be transmitted only in writing, which Plato notoriously
condemns—in writing—in the *Phaedrus*. What, if anything, can make
speech true? And how can true speech be preserved in a form—writing—
that is by definition detached from its sound? The texts studied in Plato's
Academy were all read aloud at least once (Aristotle is said to have done
the reading for twenty years); this practice may have fostered the impres-
sion of reanimating voice from its shadow. But the texts remained, and
even if readers in classical times habitually read aloud to themselves,
which is by no means certain, nothing could assure them that their speech
was more than an echo in a cave of illusion.

Plato has no answers to these questions, which constitute one version
of what is perhaps for him the most basic of all problems: how can one
distinguish true speech from the deceptions of sophistry—from rhetoric?

From the poetry he wanted kept out of the ideal city? All the while being something of a rhetorician, something of a poet, himself?

The lack of an answer is not necessarily a source of regret. It is consistent with the Socratic/Platonic principle that the truest wisdom is to know one's ignorance. That may be even truer for us than it was for Plato. The dilemma posed for him by speech is still going strong. It is stronger than ever in a world where the debasement of language, magnified by technology and pushed by ideology, has become routine. Even the truth no longer sounds true.

But perhaps sound itself is our best recourse. Plato may have thought so in creating the persona of Socrates, scripting his distinctive voice no less than the tragic playwrights of his era would do for gods and heroes. No matter the performative contradiction, the performance is what counts.

57 Speaking and Being

More or less since Plato, Western thought has relied on a division between the world of discrete phenomena conveyed through the senses and a vast substrate or continuum from which the phenomena emerge and to which they return. "Whatever may be the terms in which [this] division is articulated in the course of its history," says Giorgio Agamben, "what is decisive is that in the tradition of Western philosophy, being, like life, is always interrogated beginning with the division that traverses it."[1] That comes close to saying—and it is hard to say this otherwise—that the division is what brings being into being. At least we have not been able to conceive of being without it. The division is to be found everywhere and anywhere. We live in the cleft.

Case in point: this entry comes from the sheer serendipity of my reading Agamben on one day and an essay by Sarah Pourciau on mathematical infinities, artificial intelligence, and the "ocean" of digital data on another,[2] and then casually stumbling on a poem in the *New Yorker* by Kimiko Hahn.[3] The poem, "On Pleasing," expands metaphorically on learning to speak:

The baby laughs or sobs or sleeps and
sounds separate from noise to events,
remembered as *peas* and *appease.*
While she listens and hears

sounds separate from noise to events,
from blur to fidelity.

Hahn is in good company. So is the baby. The forms in which the division of being appears are almost as boundless as its continuum, but there is more than just serendipity in Plato's treatment of them. He turns to the topic in the *Philebus,* his dialogue on pleasing, and to illustrate the primal division—the thought of which, he says, has been passed down to us by some sort of Prometheus—he turns to language and music: primal phenomena of sound. He even takes sound into his text, using the resources of his language to evoke the pleasure of separating the sounds of music from the infinity of sound in general. We become musicians when

> we divide high and low pitch, and know the quantities of the intervals and their nature and the notes that limit the intervals, and how many arrangements of them there are—noticing these things, our ancestors instructed us their successors to call them scales, and observing other similar characteristics in physical movements they said they were to be measured and called rhythms and measure.[4]

This statement takes the sound of its own additive rhythm to measure the affinities of legacy in culture, movement in the body, and sound in music.

Why sound? Why sound yet again?

Probably because hearing is the only one of the traditional five senses that is absolutely continuous, and that therefore makes sound continuous too. If we ask which sense, if any, could make the continuum of being directly perceptible, *hearing* is the only answer. Sight does not even come close; sound does not blink. Touch might seem a plausible candidate, but touch is distributed across discontinuous surfaces. Sound is omnipresent and omnidirectional. Sound never rests. When music and language separate out from the auditory environment, they form a sensory microcosm of the separation of finite forms from the continuum. If we attune ourselves to the process, we can apprehend the division of being.

Hahn's poem is—serendipitously—one of many texts that invite such attunement through their play with language. It repeats key lines and phrases, sometimes imperfectly, as if to memorize them. It draws out unexpected affinities of meaning disclosed by the phonetic affinities linking *please, peas, appease,* and *pleas.* And in a turn of phrase worth pondering, it identifies the separation of sound from noise to events as a movement "from blur to fidelity."

"Fidelity" is a strange word here. At first it may seem to mean something like "high fidelity" or clarity of sound. On reflection, though, it suggests that what we draw from the blur demands a certain fidelity from us. When someone says "please" or pleads, or pleads by saying "please," we cannot stop with hearing what has been said. We have to do something and we have to stand by it. The act is mostly far from portentous; we can comply without thinking if someone says, "Please pass the peas." But sometimes the stakes are much higher. Not every "please" is pleasing.

Hahn's poem follows a tradition stretching from St. Augustine to Lacan in seeing the passage from infancy to fluency as the decisive moment in becoming human. It does so with a light touch, in part because the identity of the poem's baby is a blur to which the speaker aims to give fidelity. Is the baby hers or her? Is it a particular baby or just the human baby? The poem nestles these ambiguities in the latent presence of the continuum that sustains its utterance.

But it is not hard to find texts that ask for a greater share of that presence, often to excess. They do not want to tap into it but to plunge into it. By going *almost* back to the continuum itself, getting as close to its "noise" as possible without relinquishing the event; by letting verbal "music" rival utterance, they make the division of being not merely discernible but unmissable. What ordinarily appears as a separation, if it appears at all, becomes an active threshold, a thoroughfare. The temptation here is to quote from *Finnegans Wake,* but Edward Lear's "The Jumblies" will do just as well:

> They went to sea in a Sieve, they did,
>   In a Sieve they went to sea:
> In spite of all their friends could say,
> On a winter's morn, on a stormy day,
>   In a Sieve they went to sea!

And when the Sieve turned round and round,
And every one cried, "You'll all be drowned!"
They called aloud, "Our Sieve ain't big,
But we don't care a button! we don't care a fig!
   In a Sieve we'll go to sea!"
     Far and few, far and few,
        Are the lands where the Jumblies live;
     Their heads are green, and their hands are blue,
        And they went to sea in a Sieve.

The sea sailed by the Jumblies is in one of its guises the sea of sound that turns round and round in Lear's jumbled verses. And if somehow the sieve holds water, that is because the continuum of the sea divides into rhythmic language through the mesh.

And music? Just to keep up with Plato? Music can tell this story too.

The Adagio from J. S. Bach's Toccata in D Minor, BWV 913, provides a fine-grained illustration, especially when taken together with its incorporation in August Strindberg's lyrical drama *A Dream Play,* where the music is not only supposed to be heard but also to be read; the play text includes the first measure of the score. Strindberg creates a musical duel between an offstage waltz and an onstage performance of the Adagio by "ugly Edith," for whom the waltz is the sign of the world that shuns her. Just how much she plays is up to the imagination of the reader or stage director, but play she does. She plays enough to reduce the waltz to silence and cause the people around her to listen raptly to Bach.

The music involved, twenty-five measures long, is framed by bursts of rapid passagework, the defining mark of the toccata, the "touch" piece, as a genre. This is the blur before the event and after. It is music in which the harpsichord necessarily jangles, so that the blur is as much a part of the framing segments as the notes are. The event, the movement proper, unfolds over the course of some seventeen interior measures. The first ten are devoted to the unbroken repetition of a plaintive melodic-rhythmic figure that fills each measure, now in the treble, now in the bass. The remaining seven measures turn to the figure's displacement across the bar line and from there to its fragmentation and final dissolution into the closing frame passage. The music extracts the figure—a plea that nothing can appease—from the blur of passagework, then remains steadily faithful to it no matter how harsh it becomes (very), and then lets it slip back whence it came. The figure's significance rests with this fidelity to its implacable mournfulness, or, in Strindberg's case, to the "ugly" self that cannot be loved but will not be denied. Thus in this musical duel, "ugly Edith" prevails over the social and sexual allure of the waltz, but she still falls into despair—and stops playing—when a naval officer grasps one of the dancers around the waist and crying, "Come, quickly!" leads her away.

58 Minding the Senses

If you had been taking a walk and when you came back I asked you what you had seen, the question would count as ordinary.[1] It would be an expression of friendly interest. Unless your walk had been very boring, you would probably have no trouble answering. But if I had asked you what you had heard, the question would seem strange. You would probably wonder why I was asking. And unless your walk was interrupted by some unpleasant noise or commotion, you might not know what to say. "What do you hear?" is usually a question about gossip or word of mouth, not about the results of listening to the auditory environment. "What did you see?" is a question about acquiring knowledge.

This needs to change.

Both Plato and Aristotle affirmed that sight was supreme among the senses, and Aristotle introduced a hierarchy of the senses in which sight claimed first place and hearing second. This order has persisted ever since, though not without challenges and interruptions. Especially since the European Enlightenment, which grounded its ideal of knowledge in tables, charts, diagrams, and catalogs, seeing has been the default model of knowing. Darwin even gave the primacy of sight evolutionary credentials, arguing that sight assumed its high place literally, as human beings evolved, assumed an upright posture, and took their noses off the ground. Vision, moreover, requires a certain distance, which can be extended from physical to social space. The highest power comes with the best view.

But knowledge comes as much though the ear as through the eye. The point in saying so is neither to reverse the first and second place in the hierarchy of the senses nor to create parity between the two "theoretical" senses, but to do away with the idea of hierarchy altogether. All human knowledge is composite. All human senses are conceptual. All human concepts are sensory.

Consider another walk, this time a real one. Sometime around 1843 Henry David Thoreau took a walk in the snow and published an essay about it. His "A Winter Walk" seems to answer the very question—"What did you hear?—that I imagined asking instead of "What did you see?" Thoreau actually answers both questions, but in a revealing order. Hearing tends to come first, setting the conditions for seeing. What is heard gives in advance the meaning of what is seen, or, more strongly, supplies the transcendental element that the particulars of sight alone could not provide.

The essay begins with sound. It is morning. Thoreau awakens to a fresh snowfall:

> The wind has gently murmured through the blinds, or puffed with feathery softness against the windows, and occasionally sighed like a summer zephyr lifting the leaves along, the livelong night. . . . The floor creaks under our feet as we move toward the window to look abroad.[2]

Sound in the form, almost in the person, of the wind has drifted into the room with the effect, the intent, of drawing the room's inhabitant outside. And the sound has helpers: the touch of feathery softness (though nothing is touched) and the sensation of already walking, of making the floor creak and so yield as we move toward the window where the snow lies "warm as cotton or down." The room too is warm, filled with "snug cheer," but the winter cold beckons as "trees and shrubs lift white arms to the sky on every side."

As Thoreau passes through the winter soundscape, the soundscape translates into the landscape, always with the intimation of a vital, sustaining undertone pervading the whole. The landscape becomes visible in response to the hum of the world:

> The thin and frosty air conveys only the finer particles of sound to our ears, with short and sweet vibrations, as the waves subside soonest on the purest

and lightest liquids, in which gross substances sink to the bottom. They come clear and bell-like, and from a greater distance in the horizon, as if there were fewer impediments than in summer to make them faint and ragged. The ground is sonorous, like seasoned wood, and even the ordinary rural sounds are melodious, and the jingling of the ice on the trees is sweet and liquid. . . . The withdrawn and tense sky seems groined like the aisles of a cathedral, and the polished air sparkles as if there were crystals of ice floating in it.[3]

The sounds from afar resonate with sounds more near until sound is everywhere. The flow of vibration is both ethereal (pure and light) yet richly sensory (bell-like). The proliferation of sonorities becomes the medium in which the visible scene passes into the distance along the aisles of an imaginary cathedral. But the aisles, no matter that they are placed in the heavens, do not lead to a spiritual beyond but to the heightened here and now of the sparkling air, the visual translation of the jingling of the ice on the trees. The sparkling resounds.

Thoreau is best known, of course, as a freethinker and nonconformist, but perhaps his favorite way of presenting himself is as someone who knows because he knows how to listen.

59   LP: Longplayer

"Longplayer" is the name of a musical composition by Jem Finer for 234 Tibetan singing bowls. Its duration is exactly one thousand years. It has been playing in London since midnight, December 31, 1999, using recordings of the bowl sounds under the direction of a computer. When it ends at the stroke of midnight on December 31, 2999, it will start again. The work also exists in a thousand-minute version called "Longplayer Live," performed with the bowls arranged in a series of concentric circles reminiscent of the Platonic-Pythagorean model of the universe, the origin of the fabled music of the spheres. Although the live version is obviously only "a fragment of an enormous continuum," it contains every sound heard (but by whom?) in the uncut version. Its performance reflects the form of the music, which, says the Longplayer website, "works in a way somewhat akin to a system of planets, which are aligned only once every thousand years, and whose orbits meanwhile move in and out of phase with each other in constantly shifting configurations."[1] The music's mode of being thus also corresponds with the span of the mythical Platonic Year, or Great Year, the time supposedly required for the planets and fixed stars to depart from and return to the positions they occupy relative to each other on any given day. (The Great Year in this sense is purely imaginary, but there is an astronomical version in which the earth's axis traces a complete circular rotation once every 25,772 years.) In both cases a vastly extended, nonrepetitive pattern, having exhausted all of its permutations, ends by returning to its origin and at once begins again.

"Longplayer," which is also a "social organism" according to the website, and is administered by a trust, bears comparison to the great cathedrals of the Middle Ages, some of which took centuries to complete. Like the cathedrals, the sound keeps on standing, indifferent to the passage of time. The metaphor of "standing" sound reflects the paradox that the music of "Longplayer" is both never the same and always the same. Never, because the music does not repeat itself; always, because the only timbre is the "singing" of the bowls, which remains continuous no matter how much it varies in itself. The music persists with the solidity of stone.

To my ear, "Longplayer" consists of three layers of sound: the striking of the bowls, the resonance between the strokes, and the persistent ringing of vibrating metals. The resonance is the link between the other layers, the place, in this auditory solar system, of the audiable. The only expressive "content" of the music, given its changing unchangingness, is the essential futurity of its sound, and by implication of all sound: an elapsing forward that is renewed with each bell-like chime struck from one of the multitude of bowls. Taken together, the bowls form one vast meta- or mega-bowl, consistent with the concentric circles traced in the music's graphic score and materialized in the performance space of "Longplayer Live."

"Longplayer" expands on the disposition, now some two or three centuries old, to hear natural or cosmic harmony in the fluting or chiming of metal or glass, from the timbre of the glass armonica to the random harmonies of wind chimes or the Aeolian harp. For some listeners in its nineteenth century heyday, the Aeolian harp exemplified not only the animation of matter by spirit but also the revelation of spirit through matter. The pleasing spontaneous sounds gave the illusion of a cosmic order underlying random events. Placed on a windowsill to catch the wind, the harp brought home the harmony of the world. "Music by the night wind sent," wrote Percy Shelley in his "Hymn to Intellectual Beauty," "Through strings of some still instrument . . . / Gives grace and truth to life's unquiet dream."

The absence of a human player was basic to this visitation. The harp, free of our imperfections, could not sound wrong. Ralph Waldo Emerson, who kept an Aeolian harp in his window, celebrated the instrument in these terms. Here is a passage from his poem, "Maiden Speech of the Aeolian Harp," on the unwrapping of a new arrival:

> Unbind and give me to the air.
> Keep your lips or finger-tips
> For flute or spinet's dancing chips;
> I await a tenderer touch,
> I ask more or not so much:
> Give me to the atmosphere,—
> Where is the wind, my brother,—where?
> Lift the sash, lay me within,
> Lend me your ears, and I begin.
> For gentle harp to gentle hearts
> The secret of the world imparts.

Emerson wrote this poem in 1875. For the Irish physicist John Tyndall ten years earlier, the discoveries of science took the place of the revelation of secrets. Tyndall described the human body itself as a kind of Aeolian harp, the vibrations of which gave a wholly natural form to the ancient fable of cosmic harmony:

> If you open a piano and sing into it, a certain string will respond. Change the pitch of your voice; the first string ceases to vibrate, but another replies. Change again the pitch; the first two strings are silent, while another resounds. . . . And thus is sentient man sung unto by Nature, while the optic, the auditory, and other nerves of the human body are so many strings differently tuned and responsive to different forms of the universal power.[2]

This version of Aeolian music figuratively comes in classical four-part harmony, courtesy of a classical four-part analogy: the voice is in tune with the harp strings of the piano as nature is in tune with the nerve strings of the body. Each of the underlying metaphors was widespread; in the era that favored it, the little box of resonance concentrated all of them in a single place. In succeeding eras, especially after recording technology had made sound into a portable object, the same effect could be achieved, if at all, only by installations designed to occupy large spans of space or time. Examples are literally widespread, from Aristides Demetrios's gigantic Wind Harp Tower on a hilltop in San Francisco to John Grzinich's installation "Powerless Flight" in a field near Tallinn, Estonia, to the home of "Longplayer" in a nineteenth-century lighthouse at Trinity Buoy Wharf in London.

Another version of the idea behind "Longplayer" appears in John Cage's *ASLSP*, composed in 1985 for piano and in 1987 for organ as *Organ2/ASLSP (As Slow as Possible)*. Cage does not say just how slow "as slow as possible" should be. Given the mechanism of the piano, it is hard to stretch a performance of *ASLSP* beyond a little more than an hour. Notes on the piano decay; that can't be helped. But notes on an organ can sound as long as the keys or pedals are depressed, so there is virtually no lower limit to the slowness of *Organ2/ASLSP*. There have been performances of eight, twelve, and just shy of fifteen hours. But the longest performance is slated to last 659 years. It began in 2001 in the Church of St. Burchardi in Halberstadt, Germany, on an organ built for the purpose. Sandbags sustain the notes and chords until they are changed by human hands at intervals of a year or two or sometimes more.

Unlike "Longplayer," the Halberstadt version of *Organ2/ASLSP* presents listeners who do not happen to be present for a pitch change with a static, monolithic sound. At almost any moment in the performance's span of centuries, the sound represents a totality that, again unlike "Longplayer," cannot be realized microcosmically. "Longplayer" is effectively fractal; each segment that one hears exists in a self-similar relationship to the humanly inaudible whole. *ASLSP* is allegorical. Its audible segments act as signifiers of a whole that is less than the sum of its parts.

·   ·   ·   ·   ·

One more word on "Longplayer," plus a reminiscence. One reason why that *other* long-player, the 33⅓-rpm long-playing vinyl record, revolutionized listening to classical music was its retrospective impact on its predecessor, the 78-rpm shellac disk. By making it possible to get long symphonic movements, sometimes whole symphonies, on one side of one record, the LP not only filled the gaps that 78s made in the music, but it also demonstrated, by the relief it brought from manual changes or disk drops, that one role of long-form music is to make the continuity of time present and perceptible and pleasurable. "Longplayer" does the same thing on a greatly expanded scale. In that respect, it is the LP writ large.

I first encountered these technologies as a child of four or five. My paternal grandparents had an old windup Victrola in their basement, together with a stack of shellac disks. I was enthralled by the mechanism, and also by the sound of the first music I recall hearing on it, the opening movement of Nicolai Rimsky-Korsakov's *Scheherazade*. The music took up three disks, which had to be changed by hand. I was far too young to be bothered by the gaps; in fact, I enjoyed them, because changing the disks made me feel as if I were somehow making the music, personally putting its pieces together and keeping it going. The solid, heavy platters and the even heavier album from which they came helped make the music feel real. But some ten years later, when I first heard a symphonic LP—a recording of Schubert's "Unfinished" Symphony—I was taken aback by the sheer force of its continuity. The record was almost weightless and the music was all there! All I had to do was listen; the sound would take care of itself. That was the form of listening that the long-player introduced to the world.

60   Harmonies of the World

Sir Francis Bacon famously said, "There is no excellent beauty that hath not some strangeness in the proportion."[1] Most efforts to imagine cosmic harmony in the form of sound dissent from this maxim. As traditionally imagined, the harmony of the world is Milton's "undisturbéd song of pure concent"—consonance without end (entry 32).

But Johannes Kepler didn't think so. Kepler, who in 1604 changed the course of astronomy by repudiating the classical idea (accepted even by

Copernicus) that the planets moved in circular orbits, took the idea of cosmic harmony as a genuine hypothesis, not as a metaphor or myth. He even assigned to each of the six planets known to him a unique "song" that could be written out in regular musical notation.[2] Was he aware that in doing so he was giving a scientific gloss to Plato's idea that each planet was home to a "siren" who sang its distinctive note in the heavenly chorus? No matter; Kepler had another idea in mind. He wanted someone actually to compose a motet in which his scientific version of the music of the spheres would become audible. He specified the pitches available to each planetary song. He alluded to the music of Orlande de Lassus as a model for his cosmic motet. Without the supplement of sound, astronomical knowledge would be incomplete. It was necessary not only to state the truth but also to hear it.

Kepler wanted the motet to be for six voices, corresponding to the six planets. If you follow his instructions, the results are by traditional standards strange and discordant, far removed from pure concent. Kepler himself says that such consonance is very rare and may perhaps have happened only at the moment of creation.[3] Because the planets move in elliptical orbits, their pitches would change according to their distance from the sun. They would sometimes be in tune with each other, but only sometimes. Kepler adds that the pitches for the earth, *mi* and *fa*, reflect the prevalence in our world of misery and famine.[4] He looked to the motet for truth, not beauty.

In Philip Glass's opera *Kepler* (2009), the astronomer acts—more properly, *thinks*— aloud, in conjunction with six nameless soloists ranging from soprano to bass. The full compass of voices suggests the harmony made up of the songs of the six planets. (Glass avoids any one-on-one literalism.) On first encountering Kepler, this astronomical version of the ancient tragic chorus joins him in naming each planet and describing its orbit. In their climactic encounter, the planetary voices perhaps instruct, perhaps inspire, Kepler to affirm that God's creation is founded on measurement, number, and calculation: "Geometry is the model of the beauty of the world."

To take Kepler's measure, Glass unhesitatingly fits it to his own instantly recognizable style. Fair enough; he writes as he likes. But the neuroscientist and composer David Sulzer, under the pen name Dave Soldier, writes as Kepler might have wanted. Soldier tries to follow Kepler's instructions, which require intricate calculations to get the tuning right. The result is a motet for six voices complete with discordant strangeness even when, in the second movement of four, it channels Lassus. (But then Lassus was not averse to harmonies that were strange by the standard of his day.) Soldier writes that the music nonetheless has a harmony all its own. Of part 1, based on the pitches obtained closest to and furthest from the sun, he says, "We [he and Kepler] proudly show how these chords are not at all consonant, but . . . have their own sort of beauty."[5]

The strangeness of the music is consistent with Kepler's conviction that the harmony of the world was divinely ordained. The mind of God cannot be sounded. Cosmic harmony can be made audible but it can never be fully comprehensible in the musical language used to realize it. Its rigorous order is also an impenetrable mystery. But Soldier's chosen text for the motet's second movement ("Hymn to the Sun," by the fifth-century Neoplatonic philosopher Proclus, whom Kepler often quotes) welcomes the mystery— the strangeness in the proportion. The mystery nourishes life:

> The planets, girded with your ever-blooming torches,
> through unceasing and untiring dances,
> ever send life-giving drops down to dwellers on earth.[6]

In setting these lines to music, the motet shifts the grounds of their metaphor. The life-giving drops become the notes that bring cosmic harmony to earth. The music translates the life-giving dance of the planets into their song.

61   Uneven Measures

Seeing and hearing are strangely asymmetrical. It is often disturbing to see without hearing; to hear without seeing is rarely disturbing because it happens so often. Sight is more vulnerable, as the eye is. The absence of the sound that should come with a sight is a sensory amputation.

By reducing the sight to an image, the absence of sound becomes a loss of world. This loss appears as the hollowing out of distance, the deadening of the space between the eye and the object. Distance is that space into which sound vanishes and from which it emerges. Whether near or far, things seen cannot become fully present unless that space is resonant. The experience of watching from a high window as people pass in the street below is one thing with the window open and quite another with the window shut.

In contrast—but this is an oblique difference, not an opposition—sound in the absence of the sight that should come with it is mostly no more than a signal. We often process it half consciously. Only when sound is fully acousmatic, when it comes from a source that is unknown as well as unseen, does it tend to trouble us. Otherwise it is a sensory promise that, if one were to turn in the right direction or cross the right distance, the sight would be there. Sound always guarantees world. Or, more strongly: sound, and sound alone among the objects of sense, always guarantees world. There is always something inert in the image, always something animate in sound. We witness as much by ear as by eye. The image absorbs us to the extent we seem to *hear* it.

Sound from a known but unseen source may give both sensory and aesthetic pleasure—and something more. In his poem "Chopin," Gottfried Benn writes that

> anyone hearing
> certain Preludes from him,
> be it in country houses or
> at a high altitude,
> or through open French windows
> on for example the terrace of a sanatorium,
> will find it hard to forget.[1]

The music becomes hard to forget in association with the places where it is heard. The most prominent of the places in this stanza depends on the distance separating the piano in the interior of the sanatorium from the listener on the terrace. But the act of listening through the open French windows is also an act of seeing. Terraces come with a view; the distance traveled by the music to the listener who does not see its source pirouettes into the distance of what the listener does see, perhaps the high-altitude mountain scenery that the sanatorium, more "and" than "or," would be likely to look out on. The act of hearing without seeing expands into a memorable sensory fullness.

Reverse this to seeing without hearing and sensory disarray may follow. Near the end of the novel named for her, Virginia Woolf's Mrs. Dalloway, worried about growing old and moved by hearing of a young man's suicide, parts a curtain and abruptly sees "an old lady star[ing] straight at her":

> She was going to bed, in the room opposite. It was fascinating to watch her, moving about, that old lady, crossing the room, coming to the window. Could she see her? It was fascinating, with people still laughing and shouting in the drawing-room, to watch that old woman, quite quietly, going to bed. She pulled the blind now. The clock began striking. The young man had killed himself; but she did not pity him; with the clock striking the hour, one, two, three, she did not pity him, with all this going on. There! the old lady had put out her light! the whole house was dark now with this going on.[2]

The old woman is Clarissa Dalloway's double, a figure for the self she disavows or the person she might have been, but also a figure for her mortality. The fascination she experiences has no content but the bond of likeness between the two women. It amounts to the fascination of being stared at by oneself. The quiet and the dousing of the light, the darkening of the house across the way, beckon Clarissa away from the life signified to her by the noise of the party she is in the middle of giving, the clatter of which in this moment seems meaningless. Clarissa is caught between a sensory logjam and a sensory void. Just for this moment, with neither pity nor regret, she witnesses her own suicide: "She felt somehow very like him—the young man who had killed himself. She felt glad that he had done it; thrown it away."

But life persists. It persists in the form of more sound. Ironically but irresistibly, Clarissa is recalled to life by the sound of passing time: "The clock was striking. The leaden circles dissolved in the air. He made her feel the beauty; made her feel the fun. But she must go back." And she does.

62 Sound, Finitude, Music

We rely on a certain level of background noise to diffuse a sense of stability throughout ordinary life (always assuming we are lucky enough to have such a thing). We notice this most when it falters, when things become too loud or too soft, and we promptly forget it when the golden mean returns. For many of us, music fits comfortably into this sphere of medium sound. But no matter our musical tastes, we of course want music at times to rise out of the acoustic middle realm and arrest our ears, move us, sometimes enthrall or overwhelm us. The cycle of music's arising and subsiding in this way seems basic to the very concept of music. More exactly it seems to have become basic in those modern times that afford easy access to musical sound. Music in a world where music is pervasive is different from music in a world where music is intermittent. The difference is essential, not incidental. But when we install ourselves in this cycle, just what are we doing? What were people doing two centuries ago when they put Aeolian harps in their windows? Why do we ask of music what we do, and as much as we do?

One possible answer starts far afield. Notable among the many still active legacies of the Enlightenment is the rise of a modern opposite to finite human being. The traditional opposite is the eternal, the infinitely long, the defining property of the divine and of spirit. The new opposite is the incalculable, the aspect of any finite thing that can be apprehended, enjoyed, or suffered, but never fully known. The incalculable does not replace the eternal but does demote it by giving the eternal a rival, a secular double, for the first time. ("Longplayer" does that in a perfectly literal way. It even has a dedicated but desacralized clergy, the curators required to extend the performance across ten centuries—and then start over.) Where once incalculability was simply a dimension of that time that could neither be measured nor ended, the incalculable becomes the primary site of the endless and immeasurable. The material and bodily world, once the sphere of the finitude from which spirit seeks to be released, now becomes the threshold of the incalculable. From there the incalculable seeks to assume the kinds of value originally assigned to spirit but in inverse form. The truth revealed gives way to the truth reserved.

The opposition between finitude and the incalculable begins its cultural dominance when large numbers of post-Enlightenment Western subjects stop thinking of death as the site of judgment or salvation or even eternal sleep and start thinking about it as a void. Some of the most memorable dispatches from the verge of nothingness show language beating itself to sound the alarm. Thus Baudelaire jumbles, Tennyson straggles, and Theodore Roethke jingles:

En haut, en bas, partout, la profondeur, la grève,
Le silence, l'espace affreux et captivant . . .

On high, down low, all round, the abyss, the verge,
The silence, space hideous and captivating . . .[1]

(Baudelaire, "The Abyss"; Baudelaire's ellipsis inserts the abyss in sentence, line, poem, voice, mind, memory—the list goes on.)

What is it all, if we all of us end but in being our own corpse-coffins at last,
Swallow'd in Vastness, lost in Silence, drown'd in the deeps of a meaningless
    Past?[2]

(Tennyson, "Vastness"; Tennyson's last-minute, last-line answer is a refusal to cope with the question: "Peace, let it be! . . .")

Is the stair here?
Where's the stair?
"The stair's right there,
But it goes nowhere."

And the abyss? the abyss?
"The abyss you can't miss:
It's right where you are—
A step down the stair."[3]

(Roethke, "The Abyss"; Roethke's abyss is both the incalculable that we carry wherever we are *and* the void that yawns below the stair. The verse invokes vertigo, as if turning on the winding stair refashioned by Yeats from the form of Dante's purgatory: "I summon to the winding ancient stair." Vertigo: the winding comes first. But the stair is supposed to lead to a height, not an abyss. Yeats enjoins himself, "Set all your mind upon the steep ascent"—and refuses. Roethke's stair goes nowhere, as the rhyme declares. It leads down.)[4]

One familiar result of this dawn of nothingness is the cultivation, for better or worse, of earthly remedies, music prominent among them. For better or worse because the incalculable is no easier to grapple with than the eternal. The danger of self-deception is permanent. Another result, less familiar, more strange, but deeply tied up with the first, is the seemingly contradictory cultivation of self-destructiveness, derangement, symbolic self-annihilation. (Baudelaire again: "Et mon esprit, toujours du vertige hanté, / Jalouse du néant l'insensibilité"; And my spirit, haunted by vertigo incessantly, / Envies nothingness for feeling nothing.) This is the real-world form of Freud's mythical and surprisingly durable concept of the death drive: a furious resistance to what Foucault describes as biopower, the social administration of finitude under the rule of normality.[5]

And that is where music comes in. Since the same historical watershed, music has served as a pathway beyond finitude that escapes the calculable without courting self-annihilation, except in the more tractable form of self-forgetting. Music absorbs so much of its own meaning that it seems to mean, for each listener, exactly what that listener hears; the listening subject is no one but the one who listens. The result is a relationship of unusual intimacy in which, nonetheless, the music is always a step or two beyond the listener, who could—and one can *hear* this—be anyone at all. Music makes sound incalculable and carries the self along with it. The music that makes us care about it affords us this reckoning. (Just how that happens is another story.) One surmounts one's finitude for a while by identifying with the music, dissolving one's identity into the music, so that one can survive oneself just as the music does.

63 The Shards of the Infinite

The modern finitude inherited from the eighteenth century required an effort, still unfinished, to find non- or post-religious means to come to terms with its burdens. The effort turns primarily on the threat of oblivion—the subjective form of the void. The modern rise of concern with oblivion corresponds to the cultural change that turns finitude into something radical in the first place, the shift from the fear of punishment after death to the fear of personal obliteration. The most common trope for this condition is darkness. But there is another as well; it is muteness; it is being silenced. Oblivion has no voice. Not even the faintest whisper. Oblivion is the condition of absolute voicelessness.

Accordingly we counter it with voice. In the symbolic, ritual aspect of engaging with them, the arts knowingly promote the fiction that they can counter oblivion in the sense of personal obliteration by rescuing something from oblivion in the sense of being closed to perception, as if forgotten. The essential feature is that this must be able to happen repeatedly. It happens paradigmatically through voice. But it happens unevenly, in different ways, according to the media involved.

Here is a brief survey.

Roland Barthes famously wrote that by attesting "This has been," every photograph suggests that what it shows is already dead. "I can never," he adds, "see or see again in a film an actor I know to be dead without a kind of melancholy: the melancholy of Photography itself. (I experience this same emotion listening to the voice of dead singers.)"[1] Barthes is primarily thinking of photographs of people, so his comments also fit with the mortifying effects of painted portraiture, which photography magnifies because of its indexical relationship to its object. But it is interesting that his response here shifts from vision to voice.

Are Barthes's two melancholies really just the same? What a photograph shows is never present; it belongs either to the past or to a past to come. But those singing voices he mourns for are still present to the ear, really there on the recording despite the perceptible difference between their production and reproduction. They retain their identity in the sensory form of the sound, which is always a thing of the present. The same is true of the music they sing, and of music generally, vocal or not, recorded continuously or not. (In that respect Google's annoying way of identifying all pieces of music as "a song" is not mistaken.) The recording is a retrieval, not a facsimile.

The invention of sound recording transferred to a new medium the re-creative character of music, magnifying it in much the way photography did portraiture. Works of music must rest in oblivion between hearings, first via performance and subsequently via playback. Hearing them is always an act of reanimation. Recordings may transmit a sense of the past, whether of the music or the performance, but almost always held in check by the sensory force of the musical present. Music and its voices favor a "This still is" against Barthes's photographic "This has been." Recall those Victrola ads from the early days of sound recording: Caruso sings again! They tap into a fantasy we have never quite given up despite knowing better.[2]

In her poem "Localities," Rae Armantrout captures the way this fantasy slips past good sense to capture our senses. The speaker, we infer, is listening to a recording:

> It's not that I wish
> to pledge slavish devotion
> as the singer seems to do
>
> it's not that I want to be
> the object of such attention –
> but I'll listen to this song
>
> again and again.[3]

Devotion switches polarities; it is the song that becomes the object of the listener's rapt attention; love of the song replaces the love song but in so doing reanimates it. Fulfilling the mandate for repetition, the listening happens—will happen—"again and again." Such repetition follows an imperative beyond its ritual aspect. The song and the voice that sings it must be returned to oblivion in order to be retrieved again and again. Oblivion must be *played* with.[4] Armantrout again:

> A space
> "inside"
>
> can't bear
> to be un-
>
> interrupted.
> I mark it:
>
> "I"   "I"   "I"[5]

The space marked by repeated utterance, canceling the concepts of inside and outside, appears in the gaps between the short lines and in the spaces between the strokes of the triple "I." The utterance, a double affirmation, "I" and its homonym "Aye," frames an intactness that depends on rupture. The word "uninterrupted" is itself interrupted, but its long remnant, "interrupted," is an intact word. And the triple "I," which the reader can eye, is a kind of chant.

As these written-out turns of voice imply, the case of speech is tricky. For voice, the oldest and most enduring of bulwarks against oblivion is the book, which the Roman poet Horace said is more lasting than bronze. Books preserve the voices of their authors in written words, albeit most often in words that were written without having been spoken. The medium of these voices is not the heard but the half-heard. The traditional conception of them, which goes back to Aristotle, understands (alphabetic) writing as the symbolization of speech. If we read silently, we can extend that symbolization to the voice in the mind's ear, whose speech, if we summon it, is exact but imaginary. If we read aloud, we can restore speech and its sensory fullness to the symbols on the silent page. But either way the speech is a facsimile, not a retrieval.

The difference can be marked by a shift of emphasis from the half-*heard* to the *half*-heard. My treatment of this aspect of voice tends to favor the first, but the second also demands a hearing. Writing provides a surrogate for voice in the distinctiveness of style. But style is "voice"; it is never voice. Even the author's "own" voice in this context is an invention. (Whose is the I that marks the "I"?) Besides, the voice of the text may be a fiction remote from the writer's manner of speech. Yet the voice in reading does rescue something from oblivion, and does it well enough to mitigate, for the time being, the burden of finitude. Both the history of reading and the latter-day popularity of audiobooks suggest as much. The summoning up of voice dismisses, so to speak, a small piece of oblivion. Because these acts of voice can be repeated, as music can be replayed or re-performed, they escape an ephemerality that is otherwise intrinsic to voice. Sound is continuous but voice is intermittent. In everyday life it constantly slips into oblivion with no chance of retrieval. We answer oblivion with fictitious or musical voice because speaking voice is the sensory form of finitude.

64   A Passing Synthesis

Bells, singing bowls, spaces made by resonance, sound as the medium of immersive time: we have encountered them all here, and they all come together in an untitled sound sculpture by Camille Norment exhibited in New York in 2022. Jason Farago describes the installation as

> a monumental brass structure in two parts, standing alone [centered] in the empty space. The lower part is an inverted bell, a little below human adult height, with a gently flared lip like a calla lily's. Suspended just above the bell aperture is a second, elongated brass form that looks like a liquid frozen in mid-drip. The only other objects in the room are four long microphones pointed at the sculpture, which produce sonic feedback from the brass instrument, soft, sustained and sublime. The instrument is therefore less a bell than a singing bowl, its tones gently, continuously distorted by spectators' (or listeners') motions.[1]

The flared lip and arrested droplet also form a visual metaphor in which hearing an ever-imminent sound becomes the filling of a vessel. The bell shape is not only a lily but also an ear, or perhaps more exactly an ear trumpet. It makes the act of hearing visible as the event of hearing occurs.

And what does the looking listener hear? Like the singing bowls of Longplayer, despite the difference in timescale, the bell-like sound sculpture produces a continuous musical sound with no internal boundaries. As it eddies the sound merges with and amplifies the audible. Its absence of internal boundaries becomes a lived image of undivided duration, a span, accessible only to the ear, that can be sampled but not comprehended— not, that is, either fully encompassed or fully understood. This resonant duration fills the room, which holds the sound in space but not in time. The resonance shapes itself like a droplet in suspense, almost complete, almost ready to fall, but never falling.

Norment, who is also a musician, had previously sampled this sound-time via an instrumental ensemble, a trio, that articulates the unbound sound not as musical but as music. The instruments involved are all highly resonant. Their resonance spans a wide pitch spectrum running continuously from low bass to high treble: the bass supplied by an electric guitar, with its capacity for visceral and vibratory thrumming; the middle to upper range by the Hardanger fiddle, a violin-like instrument with an extra set of strings, "understrings," that are not bowed but that resonate sympathetically with the strings that are, as if a violin had been coupled with an Aeolian harp; and the upper end by Norment's own instrument, the glass armonica, the Ariel to the electric guitar's Caliban.

The ensemble is grounded, moreover, not only in resonance but also in stigma. As Norment observes, each of the three instruments has at one time or another been vilified.[2] Legend has it that when Bob Dylan switched out his acoustic guitar for an electric instrument at the Newport Folk Festival in 1965, much of the audience erupted in outrage. Exactly how noisy they were remains uncertain, but, as Greil Marcus put it, "There was anger, there was fury, there was applause, there was stunned silence, but there was a great sense of betrayal, as if something precious and delicate was being dashed to the ground and stomped."[3] The Hardanger fiddle was once known as the devil's instrument and banned from churches; its sound spurred too much bodily revelry. And the armonica's sound, as we know, was for some of its early listeners neither ethereal nor therapeutic but a nervous irritant, for some even threatening to induce madness. Norment's ensemble thus enables a music that refuses prohibition and reclaims the denied, and that does so regardless of what, exactly, it is playing at the moment.

The sound sculpture also incorporates this act of retrieval, this politics of sound, though it does so very faintly, as if to challenge the listener's attentiveness. It incorporates the equivalent of groove noise, like an understring, radio static drawn from broadcasts that Norment identifies as "community reporting and documentation of social and environmental struggles." One might say that the installation is innocent of everything but sound—which, it invites us to hear, is never wholly innocent. We ask sound to assure us of something fundamentally benign in the order of things while we ourselves are guilty, socially and environmentally, of abusing its gifts. The hovering droplet is also a giant teardrop.

65 Aeolian Visitations

In 2012 the sound artist Philip Blackburn converted telegraph poles on a mesa in Colorado Springs into "wind-powered musical instruments that whistle eerie Aeolian tones as the breeze passes across their wires." As with Norment's installation, the passage of visitors through the site created a feedback loop that continuously altered the musical environment. Blackburn's installation, however, lacked the ambivalent edge of Norment's. On behalf of acoustic innocence, it even proposed choreo-graphing the steps of the visitors, who were "invited" to wear all-white clothing.[1]

Is the same true of actual Aeolian music—music that mimics the sound of the wind harp? There is not much of it. Perhaps it is surprising that there isn't more. Only two pieces of the kind are commonly played, and one of them is Aeolian only by adoption. The latter is Chopin's Etude in A-flat, op. 25, no. 1 (1836); the former, also for piano, is Henry Cowell's "Aeolian Harp" (1923).

Chopin's piece carries the same title as a nickname, which does not come from Chopin (who never used evocative titles). Robert Schumann is often said to have made up the name, which is not quite right. But it is Schumann who made the connection, in a review of the published score, and the details are revealing.

The metaphor of the harp applies in the first instance not to the music of the first étude but to Chopin's own performance of the op. 25 collection, not necessarily on a single occasion. Schumann recalls having heard Chopin play "nearly all" of the twelve pieces. He does, however, single out the performance of no. 1 as the most remarkable. "More a poem than a study," no. 1 is also the only étude about which Schumann's review goes into musical detail, so it seems fair to extend the metaphor to the music, as the nickname has done. When such titles stick, they become part of the music. (Just ask the "Moonlight" Sonata.)

Schumann's description passes seamlessly from performance to piece: "Imagine an Aeolian harp having all the scales, and an artist's hand tossing

Example 3. Chopin, "Aeolian Harp" Etude, mm. 1-2.

these together with all kinds of fantastic embellishments, but always with a deep ground bass and a softly flowing higher voice audible—and you will have some image of his playing. . . . After the [First] Etude ended it became as if a blessed image, seen in a dream, which, already half awake, one would wish to catch again." The layering of sound in Chopin's pianism corresponds closely with the layering of instrumental voices audible in the étude. Schumann describes Chopin as blurring the étude's "small notes" to form an "undulation" of the A-flat major chord, through and throughout which "you could hear a wondrous melody in the big notes."[2] (Chopin's notation conjoins large notes for the melody with smaller ones for the "undulating" embellishment, thus visually blending the two in the score much as they audibly blend in performance. See example 3.)

Schumann also transforms the limited aural palette of the wind harp to the inclusive frame—the harp—of the piano's strings. Devotees of the Aeolian harp typically did not concern themselves with its mechanism, even though the mechanism was delicate. Sounded by the wind, the harp's strings communed directly with nature and thus formed an image, literally so, of inspiration. Schumann's metaphor reverses the image. Its Chopin transfers his fantastic imagination to the piano, inspiring it to become an Aeolian harp capable, in turn, of inspiring dreamlike states of mind.

Cowell's piece is best known for being perhaps the first to be played on the inside of the instrument, the strings of which are either strummed to produce blurred chords or plucked—played "pizzicato"—one note at a time. Melody and harmony are simple, the better to draw attention to the sonority. The melody in the strummed passages, carried by the top voice of the skein of chords, moves in a narrow compass; the pizzicato passages arpeggiate tonal triads, as if to spread out, slow down, and thus clarify the sonority of the strummed passages. There is a distinct parallelism between Cowell and Chopin, despite the difference between playing on the keys of the piano and playing on its strings. Each piece in its own way turns the tonal triad into a sphere of resonance. Chopin's concludes by making resonance itself audible in a long continuous series of A-flat-major arpeggios softly rising and falling across the full keyboard and meant to be played with the pedal down. Cowell specifies that his pizzicato passages should, similarly, be played with continuous pedal. The strummed passages are to be played without pedal except for the final chord of each, which is the triad next to be arpeggiated on the resonant plucked strings.

Cowell's piece puts together irregular parts to form a symmetrical whole, as if to embody the harp's elevation of wire and wind into natural or cosmic harmony. The music consists of four melodically identical segments, each one divided into a greater portion of strumming and a lesser of plucking. The quiet outer segments are seven measures long; the louder inner segments, six. The melody too is imperfectly symmetrical. It consists of three descending measures of repeated notes followed by two measures of changing notes. The piece begins and ends in the same key, encircling the middle segments, which are in different keys; the last segment is a literal repetition of the first.

Cowell thus brings matter and spirit together in the cyclical resonances of the hand-swept strings. But his piece notably omits any parallel to the series of bell-like high notes that impart to Chopin's étude the crystalline dreamlike quality ascribed to it by Schumann. Where Chopin is fluid, Cowell is geometrical. For Schumann, Chopin's harp is an external ear attuned to flights of sentience. For Cowell, the harp is a kind of orrery in sound, a rotating model of the planets and moons in their orbits. Nonetheless, each in its own way, both pieces call up the ideal of an innocent Aeolian music while acknowledging the element—phantasmagoria for Schumann's Chopin, fabrication for Cowell—that keeps the ideal just out of reach.

But things do not stop with Cowell in 1923, or with large outdoor installations built later to be played by the wind and the sea.

The latest and most literal version of the Aeolian harp comes from a computer program created by System Sounds, a project devoted to translating astronomical data into musical form.[3] The strings of this particular harp are the rings of Saturn. Their sound is based on a very high-resolution photograph taken by the Cassini spacecraft as it passed through the planet's rings in September 2017. The program converts the photograph into a phonograph. Although Saturn and its moons produce a complex series of resonances that reveal the composition of the planetary core, the "sonification" of the rings derives from the varicolored striations of the Cassini image. "Convert[ing] all 2 million pixels of this image into musical notes with the brighter rings producing higher pitches ... allows Cassini to strum the ring system like a harp for one last song before its fiery demise."[4]

This cosmic swan song survives the death of its singer. The program assigns each striation a pitch played by a harp. It is possible to sound individual notes by clicking at any point on the image. To release Aeolian music, however, it is necessary to relinquish control, just as it is with the wind harp. To activate continuous sound you put the program on "automatic." This setting does allow the listener to choose between major and minor modes and to set the tempo, but in one essential respect these actions are illusory. No matter what one does, the musical results are always as harmonious, as concordant, as divine harmony was long supposed to be. The color-coded notes have all been assigned to the same scale. The strangeness acknowledged by Kepler gives way to a new kind of perfect consonance. Modern science falls back on Plato and Pythagoras to sound the music of the spheres.

66   Harmonizing

But is "falling back" the right way to put it? Perhaps we would do better to ask why the effort to imagine the grand scheme of existence as a cosmos, a vast self-organizing system rather than a churning jumble, has so often taken harmonious sound as its metaphor.

A clue to an answer rests in the nature of such systems, which appear to act in a consistent way whether we are talking about ecosystems, life cycles, or individual minds and bodies. Recent efforts to explain how physiological mechanisms translate into conscious experience and vice versa—"the hard problem," as the philosopher David Chalmers called it[1]—have focused on the need to minimize the level of excitation in the system: to reduce entropy. The neuroscientist Mark Solms, drawing on the work of his colleague Karl Friston, has theorized that consciousness comes into play primarily to correct imbalances between what is inside the system and what is outside—say your body and the world around it. The mission of consciousness is to bind "free energy"; the organism wants to hover close to a resting state.[2] Solms does not hesitate to draw the logical conclusion: consciousness is undesirable. We both want and need as little of it as possible.

But how can that be true? Don't we constantly seek states of heightened intensity and awareness? Doesn't thinking itself, say about the need to limit consciousness, cultivate a high degree of consciousness? Don't we ask more of life than not to bother us?

These questions troubled one of Solms's intellectual heroes, to whom, he says, neuroscientists owe an apology, since their work turns out to support many of his ideas about consciousness, the body—and dreams. Sigmund Freud also thought that life-forms sought to keep excitation low by homeostatic means. Borrowing a term from a book on psychoanalysis by Barbara Low, he at one point called this the "nirvana principle." But Freud also understood that excitation is sought as well as shunned. He just couldn't explain why. Both his theory and Solms's fly in the face of common experience.

Or do they? Common experience suggests that we seek heightened consciousness, excitement, passion, and intensity as long as we can be confident that the excitation will return to its resting state. If it were interminable, it would be intolerable. Freud, observing that the ultimate resting state is death, asked why the organism does not simply short-circuit itself. His memorable answer was that each organism wants to die in its own way. The path back must somehow be the right one.

This principle applies both to the little deaths of endings and the big death of ending. The big death cannot be argued with. But the other journeys in life and art that aim to reach home, whether it be the place we started from or somewhere we have never been, do not end for long. No aim is final, no aim the "real" aim. Life intervenes, as life does. The value of the end, both what it means and how it feels, depends on how we understand, always incompletely, how we got there. But it also depends on the knowledge that we can never stay there. We come to rest—then come to all the rest. The sense of well-being that comes with the binding of free energy is real and distinct and transient: necessarily, desirably transient.

But what, to go home to our question, does sound as the metaphor of cosmos have to do with it? What does sound have to do with it at all?

The answer may be as simple as this: quiet. Recall that when Jean-Jacques Rousseau went searching for a condition in which he was conscious of nothing but his own being, he came to rest on the sound of a flowing stream. Quiet—not the absence of loud sound, absent though it is, but the continuous positive presence of soft sound—both supports and embodies the feeling of being "attuned" to the world and momentarily needing nothing more. Quiet is often hard to come by, but doing without it is even harder. Quiet keeps self-organizing systems humming. It does not solve the hard problem, or even come close, but quiet at its fullest makes us feel as if the problem has solved itself. For a little while we can hear ourselves being. And for a little while, that is enough.

Notes

INTRODUCTION

1. See, for example, Emily Thompson, *The Soundtrack of Modernity* (Cambridge, MA: MIT Press, 2004); Jason Camlot, *Phonopoetics: The Making of Early Literary Recordings* (Stanford, CA: Stanford University Press, 2019); Jonathan Sterne, *The Audible Past: Cultural Origins of Sound Reproduction* (Durham, NC: Duke University Press, 2003); and Nina Sun Eidsheim, *Sensing Sound: Singing and Listening as Vibrational Practice* (Durham, NC: Duke University Press, 2015) and *The Race of Sound Listening, Timbre, and Vocality in African American Music* (Durham, NC: Duke University Press, 2019).

2. Lawrence Kramer, *The Hum of the World: A Philosophy of Listening* (Berkeley: University of California Press, 2019).

3. Henry James, *The American,* ed. William Spengemann (New York: Penguin, 1986), 135.

4. Anthony Doerr, *The Shell Collector* (New York: Scribner, 2002), 160.

5. Elena Renkin, "How the Brain Allows the Deaf to Experience Music," *Nautilus,* July 22, 2022, https://nautil.us/how-the-brain-allows-the-deaf-to-feel-music-238516; Michele Friedner and Stefan Helmreich, "Sound Studies Meets Deaf Studies," *Senses & Society* 73 (2012), http://anthropology.mit.edu/sites/default/files/documents/helmreich_friedner_sound_studies_deaf_studies.pdf; Anabel Maler, "Songs for Hands: Analyzing Interactions of Sign Language

and Music," *MTO* 19 (2013), https://mtosmt.org/issues/mto.13.19.1
/mto.13.19.1.maler.html.

1. JUNE 24, 2019: THE WIND ON MARS

1. Kenneth Chang, "Hear the Sounds of Wind on Mars, Recorded by NASA's
InSight Lander," December 7, 2018, www.nytimes.com/2018/12/07/science
/mars-wind-sounds.html.

2. LISTENING FOR THE LLAMAS

1. Anne Carson, "Short Talk on Homer and John Ashbery," *New Yorker,*
December 24 & 31, 2018.

3. AUDITORY EPIPHANIES

1. This segment is drawn from my post "The Truth in Sound" on the University of California Press blog, September 19, 2019, www.ucpress.edu/blog/46462
/the-truth-in-sound/.
2. Lorraine Daston, "The *Coup d'Oeil:* On a Mode of Understanding," *Critical Inquiry* 45 (2019): 307–31.
3. Augustine, *Confessions,* trans. and ed. Albert C. Outler, book 8, chapter 12,
www.ling.upenn.edu/courses/hum100/augustinconf.pdf.

4. SOUND AND WORLD

1. Julia Kristeva, *Revolution in Poetic Language,* trans. Margaret Waller
(New York: Columbia University Press, 1984), 26–28, 204–5.
2. Augustine, *Confessions,* trans. and ed. Albert C. Outler, book 1, chapter 6,
www.ling.upenn.edu/courses/hum100/augustinconf.pdf.

5. LISTENING TO SILENCE

1. Henry James, *The Turn of the Screw,* ed. Jonathan Warren (New York: Norton Critical Editions, 2021), 20.
2. For a comprehensive account, see Kyle Gann, *No Such Thing as Silence: John Cage's 4′33″* (New Haven, CT: Yale University Press, 2010).
3. Corinna da Fonseca-Wollheim, "Review: A Haunting Tribute to Josephine Baker Arrives at the Met Museum," *New York Times,* January 18, 2019.

4. Julia Bullock, "Perle Noir: Meditations for Joséphine," https://juliabullock
.com/projects/met-residency-perle-noir-meditations-for-josephine/.

6. CALM SEA: GOING NOWHERE, HEARING NOTHING

1. Here and hereafter, poetry in the public domain that is readily available
online is printed without specific citation.

7. PRISONS OF SILENCE

1. Charles Dickens, "Philadelphia, and its Solitary Prison," chapter 7 of *American Notes* (1842), www.victorianweb.org/authors/dickens/pva/pva344.html.
2. Oscar Wilde, *The Annotated Prison Writings of Oscar Wilde*, ed. Nicholas
Frankel (Cambridge, MA: Harvard University Press, 2018), 373, 379.
3. Wilde, *The Annotated Prison Writings of Oscar Wilde*, 341.
4. Eugenia Semyonovna Ginzburg, *Journey into the Whirlwind* (New York:
Harcourt Brace Jovanovich, 1975), 198.

8. JUST ONE SOUND

1. As quoted in Simon Critchley, *Bald: 35 Philosophical Shortcuts* (New
Haven, CT: Yale University Press, 2021), 4 (Critchley's emphases removed).
2. Critchley, *Bald*, 5.
3. Critchley, *Bald*, 6.
4. T. S. Eliot, *Collected Poems: 1909-1962* (Harcourt, Brace & World, 1962),
192.

9. SONG AND SOUND

1. Jean-Jacques Rousseau, *Essai sur l'origine des langues*, in *Collection complète des oeuvres*, www.rousseauonline.ch/pdf/rousseauonline-0060.pdf; my
translation from chapter 16. "Symphony" here means any nonvocal music.
2. William Shakespeare, *Hamlet*, in *The Complete Pelican Shakespeare*, ed.
Alfred Harbage et al. (Baltimore, MD: Penguin Books, 1969), 1.1.23-29.
3. William Butler Yeats, *Collected Plays* (London: Macmillan, 1952), 377.
4. *Goethe's Faust*, trans. Walter Kaufmann (Garden City, NY: Anchor, 1963),
426 (German), 427 (English); translation modified. Goethe's wordplay takes
"Unerhörtes," the unheard-of, literally; the word also carries the sense of the outrageous or unprecedented.

10. ALREADY MUSIC

1. Virgil, *Aeneid,* trans. A. S. Kline, book 6, lines 707–9, www.poetryin translation.com/PITBR/Latin/VirgilAeneidVI.php.

11. COMING ALIVE

1. On ancient reading practices and the controversy about them, see (among many others) R. W. McCutcheon, "Silent Reading in Antiquity and the Future History of the Book," *Book History* 18 (2015): 1–32.

12. THE VOCAL TELEGRAPH

1. Herman Melville, *Typee: A Peep at Polynesian Life* (New York: Penguin, 1996), 305–6.
2. Melville, *Typee,* 44.

13. THE RAVISHED EAR

1. Quoted in Alex Ross, "The Dizzying Democratization of Baroque Music," *New Yorker,* February 18 & 25, 2019.
2. Homer, "The Odyssey: Book 13 (Poetic Translation by George Chapman)," https://allpoetry.com/poem/15544159-The-Odyssey--Book-13--Poetic-Translation-by-George-Chapman--by-Homer.

14. CAMPANILES

1. Friedrich Nietzsche, *Human, All Too Human: A Book for Free Spirits,* trans. R. J. Hollingdale (Cambridge: Cambridge University Press, 1996), aphorism 628, p. 198.

15. CANNONADES

1. Edward Gibbon, *History of the Decline and Fall of the Roman Empire,* ed. David P. Womersley (London: Penguin Books, 2000), chapter 68, part 3.
2. Gibbon, *History,* chapter 68, part 3.
3. Gibbon, *History,* chapter 68, part 3.

16. SOUNDLESS HEARING

1. Since 1975, when Edwin Gordon coined it, the technical term *audiate* has referred to the ability to hear music in the mind's ear. But it may be worth noting that when I typed the term into this note, Microsoft Word flagged it as a misspelling. What remains symptomatic is the lack of any general term for unsounded hearing.

2. Hart Crane, *Hart Crane's "The Bridge": An Annotated Edition,* ed. Lawrence Kramer (New York: Fordham University Press, 2022), 127.

3. Fiona Macdonald, "The Only Surviving Recording of Virginia Woolf," BBC.com, March 28, 2016, www.bbc.com/culture/article/20160324-the-only-surviving-recording-of-virginia-woolf.

4. "The Maid of Amsterdam," https://en.wikisource.org/wiki/The_Book_of_Navy_Songs/The_Maid_of_Amsterdam.

5. Macdonald, "The Only Surviving Recording."

17. THE TALKING DEAD

1. Quoted in Dan Piepenbring, "The Sound of a Voice That Is Still," *Paris Review,* May 7, 2015, www.theparisreview.org/blog/2015/05/07/the-sound-of-a-voice-that-is-still/.

2. Piepenbring, "The Sound of a Voice That Is Still."

20. BELLS

1. Felicia Hemans, "Oh, ye Voices Gone," from *The Winter's Wreath* (1829), https://en.wikisource.org/wiki/Poems_of_Felicia_Hemans_in_The_Winter%27s_Wreath,_1829/Song.

21. DIS/EMBODIMENT

1. "Johannes Brahms. Talks and Plays." www.youtube.com/watch?v=yRcMPxbaDAY.

2. Arthur Conan Doyle, "The Story of the Japanned Box," Arthur Conan Doyle Encyclopedia, www.arthur-conan-doyle.com/index.php/The_Story_of_the_Japanned_Box#The_Story_of_the_Japanned_Box.

3. On the posthumous marketing of Caruso's voice, see Richard Leppert, *Aesthetic Technologies of Modernity, Subjectivity, and Nature: Opera, Orchestra, Phonograph, Film* (Berkeley: University of California Press, 2015), 97–164.

22. THREADS

1. John Banville, *Snow* (Toronto: Hanover Square Press, 2020), 77.
2. Banville, *Snow*, 49.
3. James Joyce, "The Dead," The Literature Network, www.online-literature .com/james_joyce/958/.
4. Banville, *Snow*, 230.

24. SHORTHAND

1. Viktor Shklovsky, "Art as Technique," http://paradise.caltech.edu/ist4 /lectures/Viktor_Sklovski_Art_as_Technique.pdf (translation slightly modified).
2. Sandy Florian, "Phonograph," www.poetryfoundation.org/poems/57164 /phonograph-56d23a62da3ca.
3. This and the subsequent quotations are from the British Library Sound and Vision blog, https://blogs.bl.uk/sound-and-vision/2019/09/sir-isaac-pitman-phonography-and-the-phonograph.html.

25. POEMS TO MUSIC

1. Thomas Hardy, "Apostrophe to an Old Psalm Tune," in *Moments of Vision* (London: Macmillan, 1929), 8, www.gutenberg.org/files/3255/3255-h/3255-h .htm.
2. Thomas Hardy, "Lines to a Movement in Mozart's E-Flat Symphony," in *Moments of Vision*, 58.

26. GROOVES

1. Richard Flanagan, *The Narrow Road to the Deep North* (New York: Vintage International, 2015), 96.
2. Aldous Huxley, *Point Counter Point* (London: Chatto and Windus, 1954), 591–98.
3. Robert Pfaller, *Interpassivity: The Aesthetics of Delegated Enjoyment* (Edinburgh: Edinburgh University Press, 2017).

27. GROOVES II: SPACING

1. Jacques Derrida, *Of Grammatology*, trans. Gayatri Chakravorty Spivak (Baltimore, MD: Johns Hopkins University Press, 1974), 68–69; Jean-Luc

Nancy, *Expectation: Philosophy, Literature,* trans. Robert Bononno (New York: Fordham University Press, 2018), 143–45.

2. Virginia Woolf, *Between the Acts* (New York: Harcourt, 1970), 198.

3. Woolf, *Between the Acts,* 188.

4. Woolf, *Between the Acts,* 201.

28. BEYOND ANALOGY

1. Michel Foucault, *The Order of Things: an Archaeology of the Human Sciences* (1966; New York: Routledge, 2002), 17–45.

2. Kaja Silverman, *The Miracle of Analogy* (Stanford, CA: Stanford University Press, 2015), 10.

3. In *The Hum of the World: A Philosophy of Listening* (Berkeley: University of California Press, 2019), 52–53, I suggest an auditory basis for the power of referral. Jean-Luc Nancy similarly regards an auditory phenomenon, resonance, as what makes the referral of one thing to another possible; see his *Expectation: Philosophy, Literature,* trans. Robert Bononno (New York: Fordham University Press, 2018), 145–47.

29. PHONOGRAM AND GRAMOPHONE

1. On the packaging, see Jason Camlot, "The First Phonogramic Poem: Conceptions of Genre and Media Format, Circa 1888," BRANCH: Britain, Representation and Nineteenth-Century History, www.branchcollective .org/?ps_articles=jason-camlot-the-first-phonogramic-poem-conceptions-of -genre-and-media-format-circa-1888. On postcards, see Rainer E. Lotz, "Phonocards & Phonopost: History," www.lotz-verlag.de/Online-Disco-Phonocards .html.

2. Camlot, "The First Phonogramic Poem."

31. EPITHET

1. John McWhorter, *Nine Nasty Words: English in the Gutter* (New York: Penguin Random House, 2021), 173–208.

2. John Dos Passos, *Manhattan Transfer* (New York: Vintage Books, 2021), 152; the term also occurs twice elsewhere.

3. Dos Passos, *Manhattan Transfer,* copyright page.

32. MESMERIZING SOUND

1. "Concent" is an archaic term for harmoniousness—in context, for consonance, perhaps specifically the so-called perfect consonance of octaves and fifths.

2. My translation from F. F. Hurka, *Scherz und Ernst in XII. Liedern,* 2nd ed. (Dresden: P. C. Hilscher, 1789), via Google Books.

3. My translation from E. T. A. Hoffmann, "Die Automate," Zeno.org: Meine Bibliothek, www.zeno.org/Literatur/M/Hoffmann,+E.+T.+A./Erz%C3%A4hlun gen,+M%C3%A4rchen+und+Schriften/Die+Serapionsbr%C3%BCder/Zweiter +Band/Dritter+Abschnitt/Die+Automate.

4. Felicia Hemans, *Poems* (Edinburgh: William Blackwood, 1868), 42, via Google Books.

33. CATHAY

1. Amy Lowell and Florence Ayscough, *Fir-Flower Tablets: Poems Translated from the Chinese* (Boston: Houghton Mifflin, 1921), University of Pennsylvania, A Celebration of Women Writers, https://digital.library.upenn.edu/women /lowell/tablets/tablets.html.

2. Yunte Huang, "Chinese Whispers," in *The Sound of Poetry / The Poetry of Sound,* ed. Marjorie Perloff and Craig Dworkin (Chicago: University of Chicago Press, 2009), 56.

34. NIGHT. A STREET. NO LAMPS.

1. Charles Dickens, *Barnaby Rudge* (London: Chapman and Hall, 1841), chapter 16, p. 23, via Google Books.

35. THE RESONATING CURE

1. For more detail on this episode, see Harry Goldschmidt, "Schubert und kein Ende," *Beiträge zur Musikwissenschaft* 25 (1983): 288–92, Lisa Feuerzeig, "Heroines in Perversity: Marie Schmith, Animal Magnetism, and the Schubert Circle," *19th-Century Music* 21 (1997): 223–43; Maynard Solomon, *Late Beethoven* (Berkeley: University of California Press, 2003), 231–34; and my "A German Dance: Music, Mesmerism, and the Glass Armonica," in *A Companion to Sound in German-Speaking Cultures,* ed. Rolf Goebel (Rochester, NY: Camden House, 2023).

2. The painting can be seen at the website of Emanuel Von Baeyer, London, *Master Drawings and Selected Paintings* catalogue, www.evbaeyer.com/catalogues/Master-Drawings-and-selected-Paintings/schnorr/.

36. THE VOICE OF LANGUAGE

1. Martin Heidegger, "Language," in *Poetry, Language, Thought*, trans. Albert Hofstadter (New York: Harper Perennial, 1971), 188–97.

37. NOCTURNE. ANOTHER CITY.

1. Christopher Isherwood, *The Berlin Stories* (New York: New Directions, 2008), 325.

2. William Wordsworth, *The Prelude: 1799, 1805, 1850*, ed. Jonathan Wordsworth, M. H. Abrams, and Stephen Gill (New York: Norton, 1979), 1805: IX.82–85.

3. The translation is mine.

38. ANNALS OF SLAVERY: A VIOLIN

1. Solomon Northup, *Twelve Years a Slave* (Auburn, NY: Derby and Miller, 1853), chapter 15, p. 217, via Google Books.

2. Compare Frederick Douglass on the "holiday system" in *My Bondage and My Freedom* (New York: Miller, Orton & Mulligan, 1855), https://docsouth.unc.edu/neh/douglass55/douglass55.html, 255: "The holidays become part and parcel of the gross fraud, wrongs and inhumanity of slavery. Ostensibly, they are institutions of benevolence, designed to mitigate the rigors of slave life, but, practically, they are a fraud, instituted by human selfishness, the better to secure the ends of injustice and oppression. The slave's happiness is not the end sought, but, rather, the master's safety." My thanks to Michael Klein for referring me to this passage.

3. Northup, *Twelve Years a Slave*, 245.

39. THE GRAMMAR OF UNCERTAINTY

1. Ludwig Wittgenstein, *Philosophical Investigations*, trans. G. E. M. Anscombe, 2nd ed. (New York: Macmillan, 1958), no. 487, p. 137.

2. Wittgenstein, *Philosophical Investigations*. The emphasis is even stronger in the original German: "*Beschreibt* dieser Satz einen Zusammenhang

meiner Handlung mit seinem Befehl; oder macht er den Zusammenhang?" My translation tries to capture the force of Wittgenstein's beginning with the italicized keyword by inverting normal English word order. The semicolon where a comma (or nothing) should be installs a deliberately awkward pause for thought.

40. AFTERSOUNDS

1. For more on the auditory dimensions of this movement, to which I have returned often, see my *The Hum of the World: A Philosophy of Listening* (Berkeley: University of California Press, 2019), 59–60, and my *Expression and Truth* (Berkeley: University of California Press, 2012), 106–7. The sonata is commonly known as "The Tempest."

2. Quoted by John Henken, LA Philharmonic program notes to Arvo Pärt's "Tabula Rasa," www.laphil.com/musicdb/pieces/4087/tabula-rasa.

41. PERSISTENCE OF HEARING

1. John Stuart Mill, *Autobiography and Literary Essays*, ed. John M. Robson and Jack Stillinger (Milton Park, UK: Routledge, 1981), 348.

2. John Keats, "On First Looking into Chapman's Homer," lines 5–14.

42. ANNALS OF SLAVERY II: A VIGIL

1. Harriet Jacobs, *Incidents in the Life of a Slave Girl* (New York: Signet Classics, 2010), 128–29.

2. Jacobs, *Incidents in the Life of a Slave Girl*, 130.

3. Jacobs, *Incidents in the Life of a Slave Girl*, 130.

4. Jacobs, *Incidents in the Life of a Slave Girl*, 131.

43. A VOICE IN A BOX

1. David Toop, *Sinister Resonance: The Mediumship of the Listener* (London: Bloomsbury, 2010), vii.

2. On acousmatic sound in general, see Michel Chion, *The Voice in Cinema*, trans. Claudia Gorbman (New York: Columbia University Press, 1999), and Brian Kane, *Sound Unseen: Acousmatic Sound in Theory and Practice* (New York: Oxford University Press, 2014).

3. Arthur Conan Doyle, "The Story of the Japanned Box," Arthur Conan Doyle Encyclopedia, www.arthur-conan-doyle.com/index.php/The_Story_of_the_Japanned_Box#The_Story_of_the_Japanned_Box.

4. Doyle, "The Story of the Japanned Box."

44. THE CONTRALTO MYSTIQUE: INTERCESSION

1. Tom Huizenga, "A Voice Not Forgotten," NPR, May 15, 2012, www.npr.org/sections/deceptivecadence/2012/05/15/152746398/kathleen-ferrier-a-voice-not-forgotten.

2. For more on the history of the mystique, see my "Mahler's Contralto Voice," *19th-Century Music* 47 (2024): 209–218. The article, which concentrates on the sexual ambiguity of the contralto, forms a kind of diptych with this and the following entry.

3. My translation of the German text at LiederNet Archive, www.lieder.net/lieder/get_text.html?TextId=6315.

4. Friedrich Kittler, "The Melody of Birdland," in *The Truth of the Technological World*, trans. Erik Butler (Stanford, CA: Stanford University Press, 2013), 36–41.

5. My translation of the German text of Clemens Brentano, "Wiegenlied," www.deutschelyrik.de/wiegenlied.html.

6. Henry Chorley, *Thirty Years' Musical Recollections*, vol. 2 (London: Hurst and Blackett, 1862), 9, via Google Books.

7. Richard Wagner, *Das Rheingold* (Mineola: Dover Publications, 1985), 263. This is a reprint of Schott's 1873 edition.

8. George Eliot, "Armgart," in *The Poems of George Eliot* (New York: Thomas Crowell, n.d. [1884]), 324.

9. Walt Whitman, "A Contralto Voice," from *Specimen Days*, in *Complete Prose Works* (Philadelphia: David McKay, 1892), 160, https://whitmanarchive.org/published/other/CompleteProse.html.

10. Wallace Stevens, *Collected Poems* (New York: Knopf, 1954), 69.

11. William Styron, *Darkness Visible: A Memoir of Madness* (New York: Vintage, 1992), 66.

12. James L. W. West, *William Styron: A Life* (New York: Random House, 1998), 43.

13. William Styron, *Darkness Visible: A Memoir of Madness* (New York: Vintage, 1992), 66.

45. THE CONTRALTO MYSTIQUE II: DEPARTURE

1. Genesis 32:24–26 and Hosea 12:5. The story is the subject of famous paintings by Rembrandt and Delacroix and an engraving by Doré.

2. My translation of the German text at LiederNet Archive, www.lieder.net /lieder/get_text.html?TextId=4607.

3. This duality may have a specific source. Aside from observing that the symbolic associations of the rose can extend to both Christ's wounds and Dante's vision of paradise, Carl Niekerk points to the prominence of the red rose in Brentano's novella "The Story of Brave Kasperl and Lovely Annerl" (1817), which was famous in German-speaking Europe. Niekerk, *Reading Mahler: German Culture and Jewish Identity in Fin-de-Siècle Vienna* (Rochester, NY: Camden House, 2010), 94–96.

4. For those who want the formal details: The "need" statement is set in the tonic (D-flat minor, written as C-sharp minor), and the "pain" statement on the dominant seventh of E-flat (V/V). The "much rather" is set over an extended dominant (A-flat) that resolves—tentatively—only three-plus measures after the voice has finished.

5. My translation of the German text at Oxford Lieder, www.oxfordlieder.co .uk/song/2524.

6. This remains true even when the voice eventually sings the text that Mahler added to the second poem. The contralto sings both as him and for him.

46. TWO LYNCHINGS

1. It also registers as song, anticipating Du Bois's account of spirituals in the final chapter. As the riders draw near, the music of *Lohengrin* ironically segues from the Prelude to the "Wedding March," which John, for narrative reasons, could not have heard earlier. For further discussion see my *Opera and Modern Culture: Wagner and Strauss* (Berkeley: University of California Press, 2007), 61–62.

2. James Baldwin, *Going to Meet the Man* (New York: Vintage, 1995).

47. "WHITE CHRISTMAS": SAIGON, 1975

1. Ocean Vuong, "Aubade with Burning City," *Poetry Magazine*, February 2014, www.poetryfoundation.org/poetrymagazine/poems/56769/aubade -with-burning-city.

48. THE GHETTO: NEW YORK, 1904

1. Henry James, *The American Scene* (London: Chapman and Hall, 1907), 124, via www2.newpaltz.edu/~hathawar/americanscene2.html.
2. James, *The American Scene*, 139.
3. James, *The American Scene*, 131.

49. TESTIMONY

1. German text from Celan, *Gesammelte Werke in sieben Bänden*, ed. Beda Allemann and Stefan Reichert (Frankfurt am Main: Suhrkamp, 2000), ii, 76 (my translation). On the role of music in Celan see Axel Englund, *Still Songs: Music in and around the Poetry of Paul Celan* (Aldershot: Ashgate, 2013).
2. The words of the song also participate in the interplay of irony and solace. See Shoshana Felman, "In an Era of Testimony: Claude Lanzmann's *Shoah*," *Yale French Studies* 97 (2000): 103–50, at 136–42. Parts of this entry are adapted from my "Afterword: Music Genocide, and the Name," in Wojciech Klimczyk and Agata Świerzowska, eds., *Music and Genocide* (Frankfurt am Main: Peter Lang, 2015), 227–38.

50. VOICE

1. Giorgio Agamben situates the oath at the core of spoken language. See his *The Sacrament of Language: An Archaeology of the Oath*, trans. Adam Kotsko (Stanford, CA: Stanford University Press, 2010).

51. INNER SPEECH

1. Gilles Deleuze, *Essays Critical and Clinical*, trans. Daniel W. Smith and Michael A. Greco (Minneapolis: University of Minnesota Press, 1997), lv.

52. THE DEAFNESS OF NARCISSUS

1. The painting has also been attributed to a close follower of Caravaggio's, Giovanni Antonio Galli, known as Lo Spadarino. Both the museum that owns the work, the Gallerie Nazionali Barberini Corsini in Rome, and the Rijksmuseum in Amsterdam, which exhibited it in 2020, regard it as a painting by

Caravaggio. See Juliet Rix, "Caravaggio-Bernini: The Baroque in Rome," Studio International, www.studiointernational.com/caravaggio-bernini-the-baroque -in-rome-review-rijksmuseum-amsterdam, and Hubbychu, "Caravaggio," https://hubbychu.tumblr.com/post/15771530927. My thanks to Livia Galante for calling my attention to the dispute.

2. Isik Baris Fidaner, "Ego is Echocide before Ecocide," https://zizekanalysis .wordpress.com/2021/08/26/ego-is-echocide-before-ecocide-isik-baris-fidaner/.

3. Elizabeth Manchester, "Lucian Freud: *Narcissus*," Tate Museums, London, www.tate.org.uk/art/artworks/freud-narcissus-t11793.

53. SOUND IN THE MAKING

1. Walter Benjamin, *Illuminations: Essays and Reflections,* trans. Harry Zohn (New York: Schocken, 1969), 87.

54. HOUSEWARMING

1. Anna Schuleit, "The Magnificat," in The Moth, "Hearing Voices," https:// themoth.org/radio-hour/hearing-voices.

2. William Shakespeare, *As You Like It,* in *The Complete Pelican Shakespeare,* ed. Alfred Harbage et al. (Baltimore, MD: Penguin Books, 1969), 2.7.163–66.

55. LANGUAGE DEAD OR ALIVE

1. The passage (from *De Trinitate* 10.1.1) is quoted in full in Giorgio Agamben, *The End of the Poem,* trans. Daniel Heller-Roazen (Stanford, CA: Stanford University Press, 1999), 63. The translation here is mine, from the Latin text at "Augustine's *De Trinitate* Book X," www.logicmuseum.com/wiki/Authors /Augustine/On_the_Trinity/On_the_Trinity_Book_X. "Animus," the word translated as "mind," also means "soul" and "spirit."

2. W. H. Gardner and N. H. MacKenzie, eds., *The Poems of Gerard Manley Hopkins,* 4th ed. (Oxford: Oxford University Press, 1970), 60.

3. James Joyce, *Finnegan's Wake* (New York: Viking Compass, 1959), 620–21.

56. HEARING PLATO'S CAVE

1. Plato, *Republic,* trans. C. D. C. Reeve (Indianapolis: Hackett, 2004), 208–9.

57. SPEAKING AND BEING

1. Giorgio Agamben, *The Use of Bodies,* trans. Adam Kotsko (Stanford, CA: Stanford University Press, 2015), 115.
2. Sarah Pourciau, "On the Digital Ocean," *Critical Inquiry* 48, no. 2 (2022): 233–61.
3. Kimiko Hahn, "On Pleasing," *New Yorker,* January 17, 2022, 45.
4. Plato, *Philebus* (Oxford: Clarendon Press, 1975), https://eltalondeaquiles. pucp.edu.pe/wp-content/uploads/2016/02/Clarendon-Plato-Series-Plato-Phile-bus-Translated-with-Notes-and-Commentary-by-J-C-B--Gosling-Clarendon-Press-1975.pdf. Translation slightly modified.

58. MINDING THE SENSES

1. This entry is adapted from my post "Sound as a Path to Knowledge" on the University of California Press blog, March 19, 2019, www.ucpress.edu /blog/42222/sound-as-a-path-to-knowledge/.
2. Henry David Thoreau, "A Winter Walk," American Transcendentalism Web, https://archive.vcu.edu/english/engweb/transcendentalism/authors /thoreau/winterwalk.html.
3. Thoreau, "A Winter Walk," paragraph 4.

59. LP: LONGPLAYER

1. "Overview of Longplayer," https://longplayer.org/about/overview/.
2. John Tyndall, "On Radiation," https://en.wikisource.org/wiki/On_Radia-tion_(Rede_Lecture). For more on this passage and its contexts, see my "Music, Enlightenment Androids, and Modern Neuroscience," https://culturico .com/2023/12/09/music-enlightenment-androids-and-modern-neuroscience/.

60. HARMONIES OF THE WORLD

1. Sir Francis Bacon, *The Essays or Counsels, Civil and Moral* (1625), ed. Brian Vickers (Oxford: Oxford World Classics, 1999), 98.
2. Johannes Kepler, *Harmonies of the World* (1619), trans. Charles Glenn Wallis (1939; Philadelphia: Running Press, 2005), 44.
3. Kepler, *Harmonies of the World,* 45.
4. Kepler, *Harmonies of the World,* 43.
5. Dave Soldier, "Motet: Harmonies of the World," https://davesoldier.com /scores/KEPLER%20MOTET/SOLDIER%20KEPLER%20Motet%20with%20

continuo%2012.25.21.pdf. For a recording, see "Dave Soldier & Johannes Kepler: Motet: Harmonies of the World," www.youtube.com/watch?v=LOO9MzZPcKA.
    6. Soldier's translation of line 3, modified.

61. UNEVEN MEASURES

1. Text from www.babelmatrix.org/works/de/Benn,_Gottfried-1886/Chopin /hu (my translation). For a full English translation, go to www.ronnowpoetry. com/contents/benn/Chopin.html. The poem was written in 1948; the sanatorium setting alludes both to Chopin's tuberculosis and to the world of Thomas Mann's novel *The Magic Mountain*.
    2. Virginia Woolf, *Mrs Dalloway* (Oxford: Oxford World Classics, 2000), 158.

62. SOUND, FINITUDE, MUSIC

1. Charles Baudelaire, "Le Gouffre" (The Abyss), https://fleursdumal.org /poem/319. My translation.
    2. Alfred Tennyson, "Vastness," Bartleby.com, www.bartleby.com/246/396 .html.
    3. Theodore Roethke, *Collected Poems* (Garden City, NY: Doubleday, 1966), 219.
    4. W. B. Yeats, "A Dialogue of Self and Soul," *Collected Poems of W. B. Yeats* (London: Macmillan, 1967), 265.
    5. Michel Foucault, *The History of Sexuality. Vol. 1: An Introduction*, trans. Robert Hurley (New York: Vintage, 1990), 140–44.

63. THE SHARDS OF THE INFINITE

1. Roland Barthes, *Camera Lucida: Reflections on Photography*, trans. Richard Howard (New York: Hill and Wang, 1981), 79.
    2. "Caruso Sings Again" was the headline of a much-reproduced 1932 ad by RCA Victor; for discussion, see Richard Leppert, "Aesthetic Technologies," in *Aesthetic Technologies of Modernity, Subjectivity, and Nature: Opera, Orchestra, Phonograph, Film* (Berkeley: University of California Press, 2015), 118. Although the ad I have reproduced in entry 21 does not use the phrase, it makes the fantasy explicit: "The Victor Record . . . actually *is* Caruso—his own magnificent voice, with all [its] wonderful power and beauty of tone" (emphasis in original).
    3. Rae Armantrout, *Versed* (Middletown, CT: Wesleyan University Press, 2010), 22.

4. The play is reminiscent of the celebrated *fort-da* game that Freud observed in his young grandson; see Sigmund Freud, *Beyond the Pleasure Principle*, trans. James Strachey (New York: Norton, 1961), 13–17.

5. Armantrout, *Versed*, 16.

64. A PASSING SYNTHESIS

1. Jason Farago, "Camille Norment Explores New Sonic Terrains at Dia Chelsea," *New York Times*, March 17, 2022, www.nytimes.com/2022/03/17/arts/design /camille-norment-dia-chelsea.html.

2. "Camille Norment at Henie Onstad Kunstsenter," https://youtu.be /-xG-Bbshok8.

3. Dave Lifton, "Did Fans Really Boo Because Bob Dylan Went Electric at Newport?," UCR Classic Rock and Culture, https://ultimateclassicrock.com /bob-dylan-goes-electric-newport/.

65. AEOLIAN VISITATIONS

1. Karen Larkin, "Artist to Demonstrate Heller Wind Harp Installations," *Communique*, September 10, 2012, https://communique.uccs.edu/?p=7952.

2. My translations from Robert Schumann, *Gesammelte Schriften der Musik und Musiker* (Leipzig: Georg Vigand's Verlag, 1875), 254, via Google Books.

3. System Sounds, "Play Saturn's Rings," www.system-sounds.com /saturn-harp/.

4. System Sounds, "Play Saturn's Rings."

66. HARMONIZING

1. David Chalmers, "Facing Up to the Problem of Consciousness," *Journal of Consciousness Studies* 2 (1995): 200–219.

2. Mark Solms, *The Hidden Spring: A Journey to the Source of Consciousness* (New York: Norton, 2021).

Index

acousmatic sound, 77, 97, 147
Adorno, Theodore W., 7
Aeolian harp, 6, 141–142, 149, 156–160
Alboni, Marietta, 100
analogy, 66–68
Anderson, Marian, 109
Aristotle, 23, 133, 138, 154
Armantrout, Rae: "Localities," 153
Ashbery, John, 7
audiable, the, 2–3, 6, 10, 12–14, 20, 23,
    24–25, 34–35, 44, 53–54, 64, 71–72,
    78, 88–89, 92, 102, 141, 155
audiolization, 37, 40
Augustine, Saint, 9, 11, 129–132, 136
Ayscough, Florence, 78

Bach, Johann Sebastian, 65; Magnificat, 127;
    Toccata in D Minor, BWV 913, 132
Baker, Josephine, 13
Baldwin, James, 13; "Going to Meet the
    Man," 110
Banerdt, Bruce, 6
Banville, John: "Snow," 52–53
Barthes, Roland, 9, 152–153
Baudelaire, Charles, 94; "The Abyss,"
    150–151
Beethoven, Ludwig van, 14, 65, 72, 111;
    "Leonora Prohaska," 77–78; Piano

Sonata no. 17, 89–90; String Quartet
    no. 15, 62–63; Symphony no. 9,
    25
bells, 5, 34–35, 37, 48, 90, 155
Benjamin, Walter, 125–126
Benn, Gottfried: "Chopin," 147–148
Berlin, Irving: "White Christmas," 111
Blackburn, Philip, 157
Blake, William, 129
Brahms, Johannes, 51, 108; "Alto Rhapsody,"
    98–99, 103–104, 106, 109
Brentano, Clemens: "Wiegenlied" (Lullaby),
    100
Browning, Robert, 41–42, 56; "My Last
    Duchess," 84
Browning, Sarianna, 42
Bullock, Julia, 13–14

Cage, John: *ASLSP* (*As Slow as Possible*),
    143; *4'33"*, 12
Callas, Maria, 119
Camlot, Jason, 69
Caravaggio: "Narcissus," 121–124
Carson, Anne, 16
Caruso, Enrico, 51–52, 119, 153
Cassini spacecraft, 160
Cavendish, Margaret, 32–34
Cecilia, Saint, 75, 82

Founded in 1893,
UNIVERSITY OF CALIFORNIA PRESS
publishes bold, progressive books and journals
on topics in the arts, humanities, social sciences,
and natural sciences—with a focus on social
justice issues—that inspire thought and action
among readers worldwide.

The UC PRESS FOUNDATION
raises funds to uphold the press's vital role
as an independent, nonprofit publisher, and
receives philanthropic support from a wide
range of individuals and institutions—and from
committed readers like you. To learn more, visit
ucpress.edu/supportus.